The Reverb series looks at the connections between music, artists and performers, musical cultures and places. It explores how our cultural and historical understanding of times and places may help us to appreciate a wide variety of music, and vice versa.

reverb-series.co.uk
Series editor: John Scanlan

Already published

The Beatles in Hamburg
Ian Inglis

Brazilian Jive: From Samba to Bossa and Rap
David Treece

Easy Riders, Rolling Stones: On the Road in America, from Delta Blues to '70s Rock
John Scanlan

Gypsy Music: The Balkans and Beyond
Alan Ashton-Smith

Heroes: David Bowie and Berlin
Tobias Rüther

Jimi Hendrix: Soundscapes
Marie-Paule Macdonald

Neil Young: American Traveller
Martin Halliwell

Nick Drake: Dreaming England
Nathan Wiseman-Trowse

Remixology: Tracing the Dub Diaspora
Paul Sullivan

Sting: From Northern Skies to Fields of Gold
Paul Carr

Tango: Sex and Rhythm of the City
Mike Gonzalez and Marianella Yanes

Van Halen: Exuberant California, Zen Rock'n'roll
John Scanlan

STING

FROM NORTHERN SKIES TO FIELDS OF GOLD

PAUL CARR

REAKTION BOOKS

I dedicate this book to my amazing wife. Deb Carr, I simply would not have been able to do any of this without you in my life. Thank you for giving me the space to be creative – I love you. I also dedicate the book to my grandparents George and Francis, my parents Irene and Dougie, and last but certainly not least, I thank the Lord Jesus Christ for my wonderful children Harriet and Rory – I love you so much. To close, I would like to acknowledge my hometown of Newcastle; I am so proud to be a Geordie, albeit a distant one.

Published by Reaktion Books Ltd
Unit 32, Waterside
44 48 Wharf Road
London N1 7UX, UK
www.reaktionbooks.co.uk

First published 2017, reprinted 2017

Printed and bound in Great Britain by Bell & Bain, Glasgow

A catalogue record for this book is available from the British Library

ISBN 978 1 78023 813 5

CONTENTS

Sting performing with The Police in Berlin on 9 October 1983.

INTRODUCTION

In the post-progressive rock era of the late 1970s to early '80s, a three-piece ensemble called The Police emerged to be one of the most commercially successful groups of their – or any other – generation. Unlike the vast majority of bands to emerge during the punk/new-wave era of the late 1970s, the members of The Police were all seasoned musicians when they formed the group in 1977: Andy Summers (b. 1942), a decade older than his two colleagues, had performed with the likes of Eric Burdon and The Animals and The Soft Machine, while American-born Stewart Copeland (b. 1952), brother of their soon-to-be manager Miles Copeland, was already living in the UK working with the British progressive rock band Curved Air. Lead singer and bassist Gordon Sumner, also known as Sting (b. 1951), was not only the frontman of the group, but their main songwriter, progressing after The Police disbanded to forge an equally successful solo career – and becoming one of the most celebrated songwriters and recognizable voices in the history of popular music. Sting's success, however, did not occur overnight. Born in Wallsend, England, a mainly working-class area of North Tyneside, the foundations of Sting's creativity and drive for success were established in the region of his birth, with vestiges of his 'Northern Englishness' continuing to re-emerge in his music long after he left the area. Nowhere is this more apparent than in his recent solo album, *The Last Ship* (2013), a recording that formed the basis of a subsequent Broadway musical, which is replete with local dialect and real and imagined characters based on Sting's past, resulting in a vivid portrait of the time, places and spaces of his upbringing, seen through the lens of his imagination and memory. This book frames Sting's creative output against the real, imagined and idealized places and spaces he has occupied – from his time in Newcastle, through moving to London, and then to his commercial success throughout the world. It will also consider how the social and cultural conditions surrounding his upbringing in Newcastle have had an impact on his music, and how the narratives of his creative activity developed as he experienced the world. The book is not intended to be a biography, as these texts have already been documented by the likes of Christopher Sandford and Wensley Clarkson.[1] It was, however, considered important to outline Sting's early background in some detail, as it is through this that we can understand how his relationship with the northeast of England was forged, prior to it being incorporated, reflected upon and sometimes compromised. Sting's life and creativity will be discussed via a specific focus on the importance of place – ranging from his birthplace in Wallsend, to his early recordings, to his time in London and to his political activism throughout the world. The book essentially aims to provide the first appraisal of the interrelationship between Sting's working-class background in Newcastle, his musical inspiration and the places in which these phenomena took place.

As with many musicians of his generation, Sting's early interface with North American music was profound. Interestingly, in the early years especially, these influences were not via the usual blues and rock bands that were so pervasive during his youth. His early recordings are firmly positioned within the jazz canon, initially recording with a Newcastle-based, New Orleans-influenced, traditional jazz band at 21 years old, before progressing to record with a jazz big band, and then more notably a jazz-rock ensemble: Last Exit, a group that facilitated his engagement not only with fusion and more standard forms of jazz, but with Brazilian and even classical-based influences at times.

After moving to London in January 1977, the rock side of his musical personality was brought to the surface; it was at this time that he formed The Police and began working the pubs and clubs associated with the emerging punk rock movement on both sides of the Atlantic. As we will see, his move to London and subsequent frequent international travel, in addition to his will to succeed, seemed to force Sting to alter his relationship with his hometown radically, perhaps most noticeably by disguising his Geordie accent and at times dismissing his past. Despite the continued identity changes his superstardom was to herald in the years to come, his northern English roots are always there to a greater or lesser extent, framed by his attempts to escape his past in the early years, or to return to them more latterly.

The negotiation of identity is one of the main phenomena this book attempts to understand. With a musician like Sting, who has participated in so many cultural and global settings, how was it possible to avoid a complex relationship with both himself and his homeland, other than by adopting multiple identities in the public sphere? Additionally, do we consider this 'mix of identities' as being representative of who Sting *is*, or are they sharply defining who he *is not*? As stated by George Lipsitz:

> like all anti-essentialists, they [musicians] temporarily become who they are not to affirm all the more powerfully who they are so they can then move on to become something new.[2]

On a musical level, I would suggest that this comment has a particular resonance with Sting, who has incorporated a noticeably wide range of influences in his creative output.

Musicologist Philip Tagg describes how specific sounds and textures in a piece of music can allude to other styles and genres, consequently procuring 'connotations of a particular culture or environment'.[3] For example, the sitar on The Beatles' 'Within You Without You' has the potential not only to allude to the broader style known as 'Indian Raga', but to the cultural connotations surrounding it. This could include particular images of place, religious beliefs, the environments people live in, the music they play, and so on. Sting has incorporated this technique on many occasions: ranging from quoting Prokofiev in 'Russians', to using the Northumbrian pipes in 'Island of Souls' or to the use of Algerian raï singer Cheb Mami on 'Desert Rose', all of which depict distinct places for the listener.[4]

Sting's association with place is apparent not only via the varied musical sounds he has engaged with or the complex relationship he has experienced with his hometown, but in how he interfaces with the actual localities in which he makes his music. This book will therefore also examine his creative spaces – from Impulse Sound Recording Studio in his hometown of Wallsend, to the venues he has performed in throughout the world. As we will see, the location where Sting makes his music has great significance to him, be it the Buddle Arts Centre in Wallsend, where a broadcast for local Newcastle station Metro Radio took place in 1991; the Shea Stadium, in New York City, where he performed with The Police in 1983; or the National Stadium in Santiago, Chile, where an Amnesty International event took place in 1990. All of these instances are not only of historical importance, but provide important insights into Sting's personal characteristics and relationships with place.

Much of the narrative in this book lies in the borderlines between so-called facts, imagination and memories – as told by Sting, the people who knew (and know) him, the people who have written about him and the people who provide a context to understand both him and his creative output. The narrative is also, of course, reflected through the lens of my own inescapable subjectivity. Coming from Newcastle, and being from a similar social background to Sting, I have, in many ways, also attempted to engage with my own fluctuating relationship with my home-town over the last thirty years through writing this book. In my mind, after moving to London upon leaving Music College in 1984 and residing outside of the area ever since, Newcastle has become a place of my own idealized construction. I, like Sting, have found myself drifting in and out of my 'Geordieness', straddling the complex dividing line between naturally disguising my accent for both practical and class-related reasons, and feeling an intensely tribal, almost jingoistic pride of my homeland.

To date, I have seen Sting live on two occasions, the first while I was still at school in the mid-1970s, with his band Last Exit. This performance was to have a lasting impact on me. The band played two sets in what was a packed, smoky Sunday afternoon at Newcastle University Theatre Bar. Sting stood to my right, with guitarist Terry Ellis to my left. I remember the music being technical, entertaining and inspirational, one song in particular prompting me to learn Sting's bass line after I returned home. Since I had only recently started playing guitar and had never owned a bass guitar, it was, and is, the only bass line I have ever attempted to learn. For some reason, although I only heard the song (which was an instrumental) on one occasion, the bass line stuck with me – it is possible for me to quote it up to the present day. Until recently, this short, two-bar phrase was just part of my distant musical memory, mixed up with lots of other influences I was experiencing at that formative stage of my life. To my surprise, when listening to Last Exit demo recordings, there it was – in the middle of a complex jazz-rock track entitled 'Untitled Instrumental 2'. I did not remember what musical events took place before or after the Sting bass line that is so ingrained in my memory, though when I listen to it more closely, through my now-middle-aged perceptions, two things occur to me: the section is not unlike the Jimi Hendrix version of 'All Along the Watchtower', and, more importantly, the specific arpeggiated chord pattern that Sting plays has a subtle similarity to a later work – 'Message in a Bottle'. Were these the reasons this particular bass line had remained with me all these years? The chord progression somehow pointed towards Hendrix in the '60s, The Police in the late '70s and, of course, to my youth in Newcastle.

There is no doubt that Sting, on that Sunday afternoon forty years ago, had an aura about him. He was already known as 'Sting', as opposed to Gordon, and despite working full-time as a schoolteacher, he already had a highly developed sense of style – not many Geordies in the mid-1970s had the confidence to rename themselves with a single-syllable name!

My second encounter with Sting took place nearly forty years later, at the Sage in Gateshead on 25 April 2015. Sting was undertaking the second of three performances of *The Last Ship*, as part of a charity concert in benefit of the venue's tenth birthday appeal. After I purchased a ticket, an unexpected opportunity arose – I was offered a chance to meet my subject matter prior to his concert. Although the conversation was brief, I had the opportunity to discuss with Sting the complex identity issues associated with being a 'distant Geordie'. Sting stated in the conversation that 'a language has not been invented to describe the feelings', which, of course, he manages to articulate so profoundly in some of his music.[5] Despite Sting's reservations about the capacity of language to describe his sense of home, I hope this book manages to get somewhere close, in addition to articulating the important phenomena that contextualize his music.

PART 1: **NEWCASTLE**

1 EARLY YEARS

Sting, also known as Gordon Matthew Sumner, was born on
2 October 1951 in the working-class area of Wallsend, a region
of North Tyneside, around 8 km (5 miles) from the centre of
Newcastle upon Tyne, in northeast England. Five months after his
birth in a local maternity hospital on Wallsend Green, his father,
Ernest Matthew Sumner (1927–1987) is recorded in the electoral
register dated 15 March 1952 as living in a small, terraced, first-
floor flat above a shop, near the banks of the river Tyne, at 80
Station Road, Wallsend. According to Sting's birth certificate, his
parents were married at that point, so it is presumed his mother,
Audrey Cowell (1933–1987) lived there too, although this is not
recorded on the electoral register.[1]

A woman by the name of Amy Foster – who is most probably
who Sting refers to as 'auntie Amy' in his autobiography – is
also recorded as living at the address at this point.[2] Although she
was not blood-related to Sting, he reports her as being 'one of
Audrey's [his mother's] few friends', a 'well dressed' lady who
worked at the Swan Hunter shipyard – taking him to see the
'jeroboams of champagne' on launch days.[3] 'She would stand me
on the table, where the giant bottle, dressed in bright coloured
ribbons, would stand before the ceremony'.[4] After losing her
husband in the Second World War, Amy is reported in the electoral register as living alone at 80 Station Road in 1951, so the
young Sumner family appears to have lived at the address only

temporarily while they found somewhere permanent to live. Amy Foster would continue living at this address, the Sumners later moving next door in 1955. Sting reports her as being 'the first person [he] know[s] in [his] life who will die':

> 'So this is death' I say to myself, and I begin to have catastrophic fantasies, obsessing about my parents dying or that a war will suddenly break out and I will be left alone, but I do not share these thoughts with anyone else.[5]

As a contextual backdrop to these humble beginnings, the year of Sting's birth included a number of key political and cultural events which would have an impact upon his world view, such as the beginning of u.s. nuclear testing in the Nevada Desert, the Soviet Union's proclamation that Russia had created an atom bomb equal to the United States and Britain, the opening of the Royal Festival Hall in London and the publication of J. D. Salinger's

Panoramic View of Newcastle today.

The Catcher in the Rye. Themes of atomic destruction, surveillance, the linking of high/low culture and belonging/connection/alienation were subjects Sting would regularly return to in his songwriting. When one reads the various accounts of his early years, there appears to be some confusion regarding the family's movements during the first five years of Sting's life. When Sting lived at 80 Station Road, it was in close proximity to, but not 'by', the Swan Hunter shipyard, as Sting recounts in his autobiography.[6] Although there is no precise date for when they moved, his family is recorded as living at the now-demolished 35 Gerald Street in the electoral registers of 15 March 1953 and 1954 – which was 'on the banks' of the river Tyne next to the Swan Hunter shipyard. Ken Hutchinson, who went to school with Sting between 1956 and 1962, and who is now vice chairman of the Wallsend Local History Society, commented,

> it was a first floor flat about half way down the street on the east side [of Wallsend]. It was located immediately outside where the walls of the Roman Fort of *Segedunum* would have been in the area . . . It therefore falls within the Roman Empire, whereas 84 Station Road was outside the Roman Empire as it is north of Hadrian's Wall. At present the site of the former 35 Gerald Street sits on the boundary of the [*Segedunum*] Museum, [to the] north of the reconstructed Roman Bathhouse.[7]

Sting's family were listed as living next door to their original house on Station Road on 16 February 1955, at number 84, and it is for this reason that Sting reports his auntie Amy as someone who 'lived next door' in his autobiography.[8] It was soon after this move that Sting's father took over the local milk delivery business, which was located under their flat. The electoral register also reports that Sting's grandparents on his mother's side – Ernest E.

Cowell and Margaret E. Cowell – were, in fact, living at 84 Station Road three years earlier, on 15 March 1952. So it is presumed that they assisted the young family to obtain not only temporary accommodation at number 80, but a more permanent residence at number 84 – the house in which Sting lived until 1967.[9]

Sting's biographer Christopher Sandford does record the family living at Station Road, but does not mention the move to Gerald Street – a location which heralded images so key to Sting's future creative output. Another biographer, Wensley Clarkson, although confirming Sting's birth in Station Road, discusses how 'after Gordon turned six, the family moved a short distance to a flat above the small dairy his father ran on Gerald Street, still in Wallsend'.[10] Local records suggest the family moved back to Station Road in 1955, which is when his father took over the dairy. Asked about this detail, Ken Hutchinson stated,

> I don't think there was a dairy at Gerald Street, as a family friend, Tommy Close, ran the business at Station Road before he [Sting's father] took it over in 1955 or 1956.[11]

In his autobiography, which is written without a ghostwriter, Sting simply states that his 'family life began in a terraced house by Swan Hunter Shipyard,' and although he does not mention either Station Road or Gerald Street at that point, he does mention 'the dairy on Station Road' later in his account.[12] He also confirms that, in 1956, his father decided 'to leave his engineering job and take over management of a dairy', proceeding to confirm that it was purchased from 'a friend of my grandfather Ernest's . . . Tommy Close'.[13]

Whatever house he was describing, Sting summarized the conditions of his early home as 'a damp Victorian house without central heating',[14] with 'the winters of [his] memory [being] grim'.[15] This 'grimness' may have been accentuated by his parents' marital problems from when Sting was at a young age. Indeed in his autobiography, Sting discusses how the trauma involved in walking in on his mother having an affair with one of his father's employees turned him to music – as a way of coping with his resultant disturbed emotions. At the commencement of his career with The Police, Sting would be known for stating on record what appeared to be derisory comments about his hometown, declaring in 1980 that he 'came from a family of losers', and stating that he 'grew up with a pretty piss-poor family life'; he continued, 'Newcastle [was] like living in Pittsburgh . . . the whole thing for me was escape.'[16] These comments are sharply contrasted with more recent narratives, which elaborate how proud he is to be from Newcastle, and how he 'still considers it to be [his] home'.[17] Sting's complex relationship with his hometown continues to this day, and will be explored in greater detail as the book progresses.

When one travels down the full length of Station Road today towards Sting's birthplace and the river Tyne, indicative images of Sting's past include his old primary school, St Columba's and the former Buddle Arts Centre, the latter two of which are within walking distance of his old homes on Station Road. Regarding his first school, he stated, 'It was at St Columba's that I began my lifelong fascination with religion and conversely my lifelong problem with it.'[18] One cannot help but notice the number of churches when travelling down Station Road today: St Bernadette's Roman Catholic Church, the Parish Church of St John the Evangelist, Trinity Methodist Church and St Luke's Church – the current site of Wallsend Local History Society and situated opposite Sting's birthplace. Like many of the houses in the area, Sting's first home, now positioned above a Chinese Takeaway, has no garden, having instead a backyard (which at one point would have had an outside toilet) adjoining a cobbled street. Despite the large number of house demolitions that have taken place over the last thirty or more years, it is apparent that the area is still densely packed with terraced housing, which gradually becomes more built up the closer one gets to the river – a factor that makes sense, as it is here that the employees of the local shipyards would have been based.

Wallsend is in the hub of an area that has a long history – going back to Roman times, when the town represented one of the most northern points of the Roman Empire, marking the termination of one of the great cultural landmarks in northern England: Hadrian's Wall.[19] Today there are a number of signifiers of the town's Roman past, such as the Centurion Park Golf Club, Hadrian Park, The Forum shopping centre and *Segedunum* – a landmark Roman fort situated on a plateau overlooking the north bank of the river Tyne, in close proximity to Sting's old home in Gerald Street. It is close to this location that Sting would permanently document his first recordings, at Impulse Sound Recording Studio, then situated at 71 High Street West, Wallsend.

Although Sting's two houses on Station Road are only around 330 m (360 yds) from the Swan Hunter shipyard, the place where Sting arguably gained many of his profound memories of the northeastern shipbuilding landscape was at Gerald Street, which was far closer. According to Ken Hutchinson, Gerald Street was demolished in the late 1970s, having been built on top of a Roman fort, and is now within the boundaries of the *Segedunum* museum. Hutchinson confirmed that he now does a guided walk as part of the Wallsend Festival, which is inspired by Sting's early life in the area. Entitled 'A Sting in the Trail', it is based on the information Sting provides in his autobiography, supplemented by Hutchinson, who has lived in the area all of his life.

The Swan Hunter shipyard, the inspiration behind Sting's recent project *The Last Ship*, provided ongoing employment for countless generations of families in the Wallsend area for over

Sting's first home at 80 Station Road, Wallsend.

a century, between 1880 and 2006. One of the most notable shipbuilders in the world, the company was responsible for constructing more than 1,600 vessels during its peak years of production, including oil tankers, icebreakers, destroyers, submarines, cargo liners and floating docks. The close proximity of houses such as those on Gerald Street to the place where the ships were constructed and launched was not only an effective business model – enabling the workers to live within easy walking distance of their place of work – but was responsible for the floods of workers who populated the streets on their way to work. According to Sting,

> Every morning at seven a.m. the hooter was sounded in the shipyard, a mournful wail calling the workers to the river, and hundreds of men filed down our street in their overalls and work boots . . . Apart from those who work in the coal pit or

What's happening...

WALLSEND LOCAL HISTORY SOCIETY FREE GUIDED WALK

There's a new guided walk this year for the Wallsend Festival based on Sting's early life in Wallsend called 'Sting in the Trail'.

It will visit his birthplace at Segedunum his house on Station Road where his dad ran his milk deliveries from, the sites of his former schools in Carville Road, Park Road and Hedley Street, where he went to the pictures, his favourite music shop, the site of the recording studio, where he played as a child and where he performed when he was famous.

Starting at 13.00 on Saturday 5th July meeting at Wallsend Metro Station.

THE EVENT

Back for a fourth year in the historic grounds of Segedunum Roman Fort, this is a unique open-air gig for North Tyneside's 11-19 year olds to showcase their musical talent.

Come along for a chance to see the very best up and coming local musicians before anyone else. Tickets are £3 each and can be bought from Segedunum or Contact: youngmayor@northtyneside.gov.uk

Last year's winner Matty Rayson will be opening the gig which kicks off at 12 noon. The Event closes at 5pm and is exclusive for the audience of 11 to 19 year olds.

GROW & EAT NORTH TYNESIDE

Grow and Eat North Tyneside is a new service from North Tyneside Council, which is funded by the public health budget. We are very keen to develop this project, in line with the needs of residents in local communities, so why not come and join the grow and eat team to "have a grow" at producing your own fresh fruit and veggies. Also includes a free 5 a day treat for all children.

We'll be located near to the Library at the Forum site and we look forward to seeing you on Festival Saturday.

LET'S CIRCUS PRESENT 'LANDWRECKED'

Having sailed in on the recently docked SS Excess, this rowdy bunch of musical sailors are making the most of their land-leave. Expect tall tales from these tippled tars and maybe even a salutory shanty to help aid digestion. Enjoy their frivolous frollick as they explore Wallsend. www.letscircus.com

11

A Sting in the trail: Wallsend Local History Society advertisement for a free guided walk.

the rope works, everyone else in Wallsend seems to work for
Swan Hunter's.[20]

Although now a long-gone casualty of Thatcherite governmental
policy, 'for 60 years before 1914 the Durham and Northumberland
pitmen and the shipyard workers on the [rivers] Tyne and Wear
were among the most highly paid workers in the world outside
the USA, making the decline into the poverty of the inter-war
years . . . from the heights to the depths.'[21] The terraced housing,
into which Sting was born, once a bustling place of employment
that attracted workers from far outside the northeast of England,
consequently became a place of unemployment

The other main form of employment in many parts of
Newcastle during the 1950s was coal mining – Wallsend operated
several pits between 1778 and 1969, when the last pit in the area,
the Rising Sun Colliery, closed. In 1985 Sting referred to this pit as
being on 'the other side of town', although he regarded the area
he used to live in as being 'literally built on coal'.[22]

As with the shipbuilding industry, coal-mining employment
was dangerous and often intergenerational – it was not uncom-
mon for several members of the same family to be working
together – usually in incredibly difficult working conditions.[23]
Like shipbuilding, employment in coal mining was drastically
hit between the years 1957 and 1974: the northeast lost two-thirds
of its workforce during this time, when the UK government
directed a fuel policy from coal to oil. This decline was to
continue under Margaret Thatcher's Conservative government,
which which was resposnible for huge job losses in the northeast
of England across a range of industries – namely, coal, iron, steel
and shipbuilding.

After attending St Columba's Infant School in Wallsend,
Sting progressed to St Cuthbert's Grammar School in September
1963, in the Benwell area of Newcastle upon Tyne, around 11 km

The site of Swan Hunter shipyard as it is today: Sting's house on Gerald Street was located just to the right of the picture, just outside the walls of the Roman Fort.

(7 miles) from Wallsend. In order to gain entry into the all-boys school, he had to negotiate the notorious 'eleven-plus' exam successfully, which facilitated entry to one of the two main tiers of the UK's secondary school system – the prestigious grammar school and the less-favourable secondary modern. One result of the Education Act of 1944 was that access to grammar schools was instigated to provide greater opportunities for state-funded children to access an 'elite' education. Sting remembers 'the main building of the school . . . as grim and forbidding as the opening shot of a horror film', with 'over two thousand boys at the school', drawn from a wide demographic – both working and middle class, including 'sons of Catholic doctors, lawyers . . .

thrown together with the sons of coal miners, shipyard and factory workers – and one milkman's son'.[24] He also recalled being

> invited to large detached homes surrounded by landscaped gardens, with two-car garages, walk-in refrigerators, paintings and books, stereo systems, and all the accoutrements of the burgeoning middle classes.[25]

Sting remembers St Cuthbert's as an all-boys Catholic school, led by a 'group of priests', the headmaster being as 'fearsome a man of God as ever walked in a black cloak'.[26] In his autobiography, Sting recounts the details of regularly being caned, which may be one of the factors accounting for his lifelong 'problem with religion'. Other teachers in the school are depicted as having an aura not unlike professor Severus Snape in the *Harry Potter* films: 'a black gown hangs loosely over a grey three-piece suit moulded closely to the angular wire of his body', with his 'pitiless eyes observing and passing sentence on the world below'.[27] Interestingly, the person behind this terrifying portrayal, the literature teacher, is the same individual who facilitated Sting's interest in prose:

> He will guide us through the barren landscapes of Eliot's *The Waste Land*, Dante's *Purgatorio*, and the hellfire of Joyce's *A Portrait of the Artist as a Young Man*. He will help us uncover the human tragedies of Shakespeare and the petty moral foibles of Chaucer's *Canterbury Tales*.[28]

When interviewed, novelist Tony Bianchi – who attended St Cuthbert's Grammar School with Sting – had some fascinating insights into the environment in which children at the school studied. First, he felt it important to point out that around a year prior to starting school, the Second Vatican Council (sometimes referred to as 'Vatican II') began its formal consultation process on 11 October 1962 under Pope John XXIII – culminating three years later under Pope Paul VI in 1965. The objective of the council was to reconsider the relationships between the Roman Catholic Church and the modern world, with changes including moderating the notion of the Catholic Church alone bringing salvation to mankind, the introduction of laity into the class-room, the use of local language in holy mass (as opposed to Latin) and a concerted attempt at a more open dialogue with other Christian religions. During the first three years of Sting's time at St Cuthbert's, changes such as these were being imple-mented and assimilated, with the school attempting to make sense of the increased liberalism.

> Bianchi: The older generation there, especially the clerics, belonged to the old world – you know 'hell fire and damna-tion'. We had retreats every year in the school, with Jesuits coming in telling you that you would burn forever if you didn't go to mass on Sunday . . . You would also go off to Sunderland for an annual Easter retreat, and be in total silence for three days.[29]

Confirming Sting's earlier description (above) regarding the fearful images of some of the priests, Bianchi elaborated:

> Some of them [the Priests] had pretty nasty streaks in them. You suspect they would have been people tempted toward any position of authority, and they were distinctly ill suited to the role. They adhered to the old church views – having a mono-poly on the truth, righteousness etc. I saw a priest punch one child to the floor. He [looked] like a skeleton, clothed in black, and he would parade along the terrace.[30]

Bianchi was quick to point out that

> The 'terrors' amongst the kids and the priests were in the
> minority – but of course it is these that get mythologized.
> We're talking class mythology and Catholic mythology –
> and people project themselves against this backdrop.[31]

Although he was not part of Sting's friendship group, Bianchi
remembers him as being 'slightly set apart and aloof', although he
conceded that this is based on 'one's tendency as a child to make
very quick impressions – and they tend to stick [whether they are
correct or not]'.[32] Discussing the above-mentioned mythology,
he suggested that Sting himself has a tendency to undertake a
'celebration of this working class background'. It's not that it's
false, just partial, where he is romanticizing himself against this
'alien' environment.[33]

    This leads to larger questions of how Sting, or indeed anyone,
defines personal identity. In order to do this, it appears that at
least part is formulated by going back to previous generations.
In Sting's case, it is going back to the working-class values of his
father, resulting in the locus of the 'ship at the bottom of the
street'. With Sting's departure from the Wallsend area in 1967, his
perspective can be considered part of what one author describes
as 'the invention of tradition' – 'to compensate for factors of
identity that have been taken away'.[34]

    Sting graduated from St Cuthbert's in 1970 with A Levels in
English Literature, Geography and Economics, and by that time
he had developed a strong interest in music. Having inherited a
rundown acoustic guitar from his uncle around 1962, he was to
purchase his first new acoustic instrument in Braidfords Music
Shop, Wallsend. Although no precise date is given – it appears that
Sting became interested in the bass guitar shortly before he took
his A Levels – when he stepped in to replace a friend on a gig,

Sting and his classmates (including Tony Bianchi) at St Cuthbert's Grammar School in May 1964.

Sting (middle row, fourth from right) and his classmates at St Cuthbert's Grammar School, May 1970.

he decided 'the bass, while being far from flashy, would suit the covert side of [his] personality much better than the guitar.'[35] After an ill-fated attempt studying English at Warwick University near Coventry, Sting left after just one term and undertook a number of jobs, including bus conductor, building site labourer and tax officer, before eventually deciding to attend the Northern Counties Teacher Training College between 1971 and 1974. It was here that Sting was to begin playing bass regularly, eventually forming the band Last Exit and performing on a freelance basis, including stints with the Newcastle Big Band and the Phoenix Jazzmen.

It was during this time that he received his famous nickname, reportedly from Gordon Solomon when playing with the Newcastle Big Band, because of his tendency to wear a horizontally striped yellow-and-black jumper, which supposedly made him resemble a bee. Although the suggestion was a throwaway comment at the time, it was to align him with other rock/pop musicians who have adopted single-name aliases – such as Slash (from Guns 'N Roses), Bono (from U2), Flea (from the Red Hot Chili Peppers), Suggs (from Madness), Pink and Lemmy (from Motörhead), all of whom had their stage names prior to forming their respective music careers – the new names normally describing aspects of their characters.[36] For example, Bono comes from the Latin *bonavox* – meaning 'good voice', Flea was based on a 'cartoon' name a friend gave him and Slash was so-named because he was always hustling and in a hurry. In Sting's case, the name no longer simply describes what he used to wear, but is now effectively a 'trademark', which differentiates him from his 'old self'. After forming The Police, the personality differences between Gordon Sumner and 'Sting' were to become more profound; these will be the subject of the next chapter.

Screenshot from *The Stars Look Down* (1940).

2 MAN IN A SUITCASE

We called ourselves 'Geordies' for historical reasons that are
still debated by local historians but have been forgotten by
most of us.[1]

The Welsh word *hiraeth*, in spite of having no direct English
translation, arguably describes the complex 'feelings' felt by many
Geordies who have left their homeland. Described as combining
homesickness, grief and sadness with an intense pride of home,
it is possibly this feeling that has fuelled much of Sting's work on
The Soul Cages and his recent creative activity on *The Last Ship*.
In order to get inside Sting's thought processes, it is interesting
to consider the means through which many of us put on metaphorical masks when faced with new situations and opportunities
– masks that may strongly conflict with the aforementioned
feelings or even our personal characteristics. This is particularly
the case in the entertainment industry, in which the personas of
many stars are distinct from who they are in real life. This creative
tension – between the 'real person' and a distinct persona – has
resulted in inspired music from countless artists throughout the
history of popular music.[2] However, it could be argued that no
artist has engaged in this process in quite the same way as Sting,
who has participated in a fascinating journey over the last forty
years when portraying his northern English identity.

As indicated by Sting, the meaning of the term 'Geordie' is
indeed debated: historians Robert Colls and Bill Lancaster assert,
'there is no definitive meaning to the name anyway.'[3] These
authors provide a number of disputed meanings for the word,
such as 'a name given to coalminers', 'a term for the Tyneside

dialect' and 'people born within three miles of the banks of the [river] Tyne from South Shields to Hexham'.[4] This ambiguity resonates with the depictions of the region by the media, which describe it as 'grim' or 'spectacular', 'amusing' or 'threatening', 'artistic' or 'unqualified' – with 'grim', 'threatening' and 'unqualified' often taking the dominant position. One need only look at Sting's biographers' depictions of his background to see examples of this narrative: 'All around lay miles of drab, quarried hills, slag-heaps and allotments'; 'How many children from a background of backstreet slums and near poverty have made it to the top in any decade this century?'[5] Even Sting, especially in his early relationship with his hometown, had a tendency to play on this narrative. However, placing these statements into context, regions such as Newcastle are also 'imagined communities': 'Who the Geordies are depends on who they imagine themselves to be', with 'belonging' being 'an act of affiliation not of birth'.[6] It is suggested that this affiliation is particularly important when considering Sting, who has not lived in the area for forty years. However, he has continued to visit the area both physically and via his music. Examples of him visiting/interfacing with his home city are numerous, ranging from engaging in educational support in institutions such as Newcastle College, special concerts, local movie-making, performing with homegrown musicians, receiving honorary doctorates and commissioning works of art, through to investing in local companies such as Amazing Media.[7] As we will discover, songs such as 'We Work the Black Seam', and in particular albums such as *The Soul Cages*, *If on a Winter's Night . . .* and *The Last Ship* have interacted directly with a 'Newcastle narrative'.

Connecting with his hometown is something that Sting has used not only to exorcize the ghosts of his past, but to assist with two extended occurrences of writer's block – the two factors being seemingly intertwined. In 1991 he stated,

For almost three years, I hadn't written even one rhyming
couplet. I'd written a lot of little fragments of music,
but there were no real ideas coming out. I was genuinely
frightened.[8]

In his *Lyrics* book, Sting elaborated on the potential reasons for his
creativity disappearing and then re-emerging, linking both firmly
to his past in Newcastle:

My father died in 1989. We'd had a difficult relationship, and
his death hit me harder than I'd imagined possible. I felt
emotionally and creatively paralysed, isolated and unable
to mourn. I just felt numb and empty, as if the joy had been
leached out of my life. Eventually I talked myself into going
back to work, and this sombre collection of songs [*The Soul
Cages*] was the result. I became obsessed with my hometown
and its history, images of boats and the sea, and my childhood
in the shadow of the shipyards.[9]

In another 1991 article, he continued,

As soon as I remembered the first memory of my life,
everything started to flow. The first memory was of a ship,
because I lived next to a shipyard when I was young. It was
a very powerful image of this huge ship towering above the
house. Tapping into that was a godsend. I began with that,
and the album just flowed. It was written in about three or
four weeks.[10]

Twelve years later, in 2003, after recording four more albums,
culminating in *Sacred Love*, he found his songwriting had once
again begun to dry up – seemingly, he was no longer interested in
the 'self-obsession that goes with songwriting'. He continued: 'at

Sting at the Central Station in Newcastle, when The Police performed two concerts at Newcastle City Hall on 28th April 1980, in support of Northumberland Association of Boys' Clubs.

a certain point it's tiring. And then of course, there's the public scrutiny of those revelations that you made.'[11] Consequently, in the ten years between *Sacred Love* and *The Last Ship*, Sting focused on recording the songs of English Renaissance composer John Dowland (*Songs from the Labyrinth*, 2006), a collection of traditional and classical songs associated with winter (*If on a Winter's Night . . .*, 2009), classical adaptations of his past portfolio (*Symphonicities*, 2010) and remixes of his greatest hits (*The Best of 25 Years*, 2011), in addition to the record-breaking reunion tour by The Police in 2007–8.

Speaking at a public lecture in 2014, after informing his audience of his early life living next door to the shipyard and his dreams of becoming a successful songwriter, he commented,

Then one day, the songs stopped coming . . . day after day you face a blank page and nothing's coming – and those days turn into weeks, and weeks to months, and pretty soon those months have turned into years, with very little to show for your efforts – no songs.[12]

As with *The Soul Cages* more than twenty years before, Sting once again reflected on how his hometown became the antidote to his writer's block:

it's ironic that the landscape that I worked so hard to escape from and the community that I more or less abandoned and exiled myself from should be the very landscape, the very community I would have to return to to find my missing muse.[13]

Regarding the impact of Sting's music on the public perception of Newcastle, 'most people outside the North and many people within it have come to know the region not through personal experience, but by the versions they encounter in the field of culture',[14] with TV personalities such as Ant and Dec and Jimmy Nail, films such as *Get Carter* (1971) and *Billy Elliot* (2000), and TV programmes such as *When the Boat Comes in* (1976–81), *The Likely Lads* (1964–6) and *Auf Wiedersehen, Pet* (1983–4, 1986, 2002) all conjuring up images of what it means to be a Geordie in the national imagination.[15] Although it could be argued that Sting is continuing these narratives in *The Last Ship* in particular, on a personal level, being wealthy, a world traveller, educated and literate, he breaks away from many of the stereotypes. As in numerous northern regions in the UK, the Geordie identity is often contrasted against that of London, with the overarching British identity considered southeast-centric by academics such as Martin Weiner, who argued that the dominant classes 'sought to construct a distinctive and defensive type of Englishness . . . in which the south of England has often stood proxy for the nation as a whole'.[16] This is a position that became more profound after the rise of Thatcherism – Thatcher inadvertently placed this division on the agenda again when she attacked trade unionism and instigated the privatization of industry, a subject Sting would deal with in 'We Work the Black Seam'.

The alienation of the northeast of England, considered as inferior or purely localized, is also apparent in the art world, the Ashington Group of artists – mainly working miners based in the area between the mid-1930s and 1980s – usually regarded by the establishment as producing 'simple expression under unlikely conditions':[17]

> [their] art could not be reflective: it had to be primitive, without thought. As painters who stayed in the region in their homes, in their jobs, their art could not address the universal: it had to be provincial.[18]

The seeming inability of the northeast actually to know and represent *itself* was reflected in films such as *The Stars Look Down* (1940), which although set in the Northumberland mines of Tynecastle (Newcastle) and featuring the occasional authentic named place such as Jesmond Dene and Westgate Road, did not feature any local actors, was not set in the region and consisted of Geordie accents that were not recognizably from the area.[19] As Colls continued,

> the working class painter or author was virtually a contra-diction in terms in some circles – this meant someone who inevitably looks back, back at what he had been but no longer was.[20]

Although it could be argued that much of Sting's Newcastle-based music complies with this narrative, the Broadway appearance of *The Last Ship*, in addition to the popularity of recordings such as *The Soul Cages* and *If on a Winter's Night . . .* indicate that his more localized narratives also have some universal appeal.[21]

Identity portrayed through music has a long history – composers such as Sibelius and Grieg typified the 'nationalism' movement of the nineteenth century. This has continued in popular music, with artists such as The Proclaimers from Scotland, The Super Furry Animals from Wales, Bruce Springsteen from the United States and U2 from Ireland, all displaying their national identities via music in a variety of ways. Although Sting is not necessarily displaying a national identity, he is representing a northern English one in works such as *The Last Ship,* which is a similar phenomenon. Artists such as Sting can be considered to have multiple identities, which are, in part, related to their relationships and interactions with other people, each interaction potentially leading to a new identity. These identities can often be contradictory – 'for example a musician can be a "different person" on stage than when in solitary rehearsals, and be different again when engaged in a number of non-musical activities.'[22] Identities alter *through time* and in different ways, and this is certainly the case with Sting. Asked about how Sting has changed over the years, his long-time friend John Hedley commented, 'His whole character has changed drastically since those [Last Exit] days.'[23] Sting's broader relationship with Newcastle is indicative of this process – he has adopted a very positive position today compared to his negative comments in the late '70s to early '80s. Asked in 2009 about his changing perspective of his hometown, he commented,

> I think I am at the time of my life when I can come back here and put my life into perspective by returning to where it began, and make much more sense of it . . . meeting friends

and dealing with ghosts of the past . . . there's a lot of ghosts in my life.[24]

In the same interview, which took place in The Cumberland Arms in Byker, a short distance from where Sting grew up, he was asked if his music had a regional identity 'running all the way through it'. Sting responded,

> My interest is in creating a synthesis much wider than a regional identity, it's an international thing, it's a World Music if you like. But in order for that to make sense it has to have some beginning and some roots – and it's here [Newcastle]. It's a fierce regional pride, a way of singing that I think is unique to Geordies. We sing in a certain way.[25]

Although initially known locally as a jazz musician, and then becoming widely known through latching on to a punk/new wave identity, Sting has been able to construct further versions of himself after commencing his first solo album, *The Dream of the Blue Turtles*, in which the very act of performing with esteemed jazz musicians such as Branford Marsalis and Kenny Kirkland imbued him with the identity of a 'schooled' musician, who has knowledge, interest and a musical ability that resonates with jazz, while still remaining commercially appealing. Having come out of what was essentially a rock and roll band, Sting obviously felt that this additional dimension to his identity was important. Discussing the impact of the musicians he hired, he commented on how the new project made his position as the main creative force clearer: 'I hired them to play, and I'm the songwriter and singer. So there are no arguments about roles, which makes the process a lot easier.'[26] It is obvious that working with esteemed jazz musicians also pushed him musically, seeming initially to challenge his confidence. During the recording of the album, he commented, 'My voice, it's so weak. I was even tearful before. I just wanted to forget the band. I wanted to go home, crawl into bed, just forget the whole thing because I can't sing.'[27] However, this comment was followed with the confident assertion that 'on this record I've recruited some of the best young players in America but I think I'm the best songwriter, so I'm not being immodest, the band has a good pedigree, and I'm part of the pedigree.'[28] It also appears that the new adventure highlighted the importance of Sting's need to be seen differently: 'as soon as they're sure about who you are and what you're gonna come up with next, then you're dead, stagnant and useless.'[29] In addition to *The Dream of the Blue Turtles* displaying an affinity with his native northeast through 'We Work the Black Seam', it also gave him the opportunity to deal with a range of other cultural and social identities such as the Caribbean ('Love is the Seventh Wave'), the Soviet Union ('Russians') and London ('Children's Crusade'), as well as personal relationships ('If You Love Somebody Set Them Free' and 'Consider Me Gone'). As the years progressed, Sting was to extend the complexity of his identity to include someone who understood and often combined ingredients such as the tradition of the songwriter when performing the music of John Dowland (*Songs From the Labyrinth*, 2006), political activism, classical music, the exorcism of his past and engagement in the musical theatre tradition.[30]

Considering why Sting implements such a broad range of musical identities in his music, there are three possible interrelated explanations: 1) he wishes to portray these identities to the general public to *display* his musical expertise, political convictions, intelligence, working-class background, and so on; 2) we accept the notion that musical taste changes with both age and social standing, in addition to being affected by life circumstances; or, finally, 3) Sting has an ingrained psychological need to prove how far he has travelled since his early days in Wallsend. We could say we have simply witnessed Sting growing up!

Central to the perception of Sting's musical identity is the range of performance environments he has encountered during this time (ranging from small local pubs to large football stadiums), in addition to the multiple roles he has engaged with, such as rock star, jazz musician, bass player, composer, songwriter, teacher, Geordie, and so on – all of which have social and cultural connotations. Many of these positions have social currency, with 'the hierarchy of musicianship elevating the originators of music – the authors, if you like – above those whose role is merely one of reproduction, in other words the performers'.[31]

In an interview in 1983 for *Rolling Stone*, Sting reflected on the impacts of stardom on his personal characteristics, stating,

> I'm quite interested in finding me again . . . I used to be the same sort of person on-stage that I was in private life, but now it's sort of a monster. He looks wonderful with the lights and the crowds, but in the kitchen, it's a bit much. I'm just trying to find out who is the real me – is it this monster or someone more normal? Right now, he's a bit worn at the edges.[32]

Sting's reference to himself as 'he' in this interview is interesting, as, like many successful rock stars before him, he can be considered to have developed a complex persona, in which he held there to be a clear difference between local boy Gordon Sumner and the rock star the world knows as 'Sting'. According to Sting's biographer Christopher Sandford, both his then-wife Frances Tomelty and his young son Joe were asked to call him by his stage name as early as 1980 – something which can be verified in his autobiographical movie *Bring on the Night* (1985), in which he was clearly offended when a journalist called him 'Gordon' during a press conference, asking, 'Who is this Gordon Sumner character?'[33] This narrative was also verified by his second wife Trudie Styler, who stated,

> I don't know who this Gordon Sumner is – I have never
> lived with Gordon Sumner. It's not been a name that has
> ever been used in the house. He is two Stings. He is Sting
> the professional . . . and he is Sting, you know dad and
> husband.[34]

Commenting on his personality in the early 1980s, the 31-year-old
Sting described the dual nature of his character, stating, 'I am sort
of two people . . . and I do have a dark side.'[35] So considering his
creative output, the complexities of Sting's character and identity
outlined above should theoretically be visible in his music, something which Sting confirmed:

> My personal life is in my songs . . . Many of them seem quite
> contradictory and I seem to be two people: on the one hand,
> a morose, doom-laden character, and on the other, a happy-
> go-lucky maniac. I am as ambiguous as Martin, the character
> I played in 'Brimstone and Treacle', and I didn't have to delve
> too deeply into myself to excavate him. He's definitely an
> exaggerated version of me.[36]

Sting has discussed how, as a songwriter, he enjoys the notion
of having dark subject matter juxtaposed with 'jolly' music.[37] As
an example, this philosophy pervades his work from *Outlandos
d'Amour* on, with songs such as 'Next to You', 'Be My Girl – Sally'
and 'Can't Stand Losing You', as well as the chorus of 'So Lonely',
through to later songs such as 'All This Time', all clearly realizing
this 'split personality' objective. However, happy and sad emotions
can be defined against each other, but not necessarily in a way
that suggests a split personality. If we consider these feelings to
be co-present in the *same emotional space*, it is possible to position
any sadness in direct relation to happiness, and vice versa. This
can result in phrases from the aforementioned songs describing

Sting playing the part of Martin in *Brimstone and Treacle*.

feelings such as 'angry happiness' or 'passionate need'. When one
reads songs such as these from this viewpoint, the singer of a song
is not experiencing two separate emotions, but a complex version
of the same one. Discussing the issues associated with attempting
to comprehend two distinct conversations taking place in every-
day conversation, composer Jean-Claude Risset alluded to how we
usually have to 'extract one and ignore the others, but in music
we can listen to different voices simultaneously'.[38] Relating this to
Sting, the 'voices' that Risset is alluding to could be the musical
backing *and* the lyrics – resulting in an emotional response that
is more profound than listening to words only. The fact that an
emotional response is taking place beyond the lyrics confirms
that something is taking place in terms of the information being

imparted. The question is, what? It is suggested that this combination of lyrics and sound provides further clarification of *who* is singing the song.

This leads to a question – how can we use Sting's music to understand his creativity, identity and personality better? As opposed to solely attempting to get to know the actual 'singer' of a piece of music, it is useful to consider the broader persona of an artist – these factors are often distinct and interrelated; the distinctions between the 'real person' (that is, Gordon Sumner), the 'performance persona' (Sting) and the 'character(s)' in the text/lyrics are key.[39] This, in turn, leads to a number of important considerations, such as the relationship between the real person and the persona; whether the character of a song is based on real or imagined characters in the singer's life; how and why the characters interact with one another; and how the musical textures of a piece of music relate to all of this. These often complex relationships have potential impacts on us as listeners; they enable us to respond either passively (the song has no impact on us), or actively, in which we can actually inhabit the lyrics of the song.

A song such as 'Dead Man's Boots' from *The Last Ship* (2013) can be seen to include a number of characters, all of which are related to Sting's past. The song commences with a father speaking to his son, Gideon. However, although on one level this is simply a dialogue between characters in the 'script' of *The Last Ship*, it can also be considered autobiographical – the 'father' can easily be seen to be addressing the young Gordon Sumner. This parallel dialogue can therefore be considered as either fictional, where the father-to-son dialogue can be read as being between two characters, or real, in which the interchange is an allegory for a conversation between two actual people: Sting and his father. Interestingly, the second verse of the song progresses from what is thus far a private conversation between father and son, to a narrative that is more social in nature, in which the real person or persona (be it Gordon Sumner or his alter ego Sting) – or indeed, the fictional character (the son / Gideon) – is now telling us as listeners a story. This shift in emphasis, which is essentially a recollection of a father, has the impact of including the listener in the narrative more directly, giving us the potential to inhabit one of the characters in the song. This is something that has affected me personally – having a similar social back-ground and northeastern heritage to Sting, it is easy to identify with either the son character as myself, or the father character as my grandfather. After the second chorus is repeated, the song shifts to a bridge section, delivered by the son, who this time asks the audience why he would agree with his father's point of view. Once again, because it is a statement to us as listeners, it can be considered a development of the song's social nature, and can again be viewed as an announcement from the character Gideon, the real person Gordon Sumner, the persona Sting or indeed us, depending on how one interprets it.

In addition to these perspectives, this voicing of the 'son's' complex relationship with his 'father' could be viewed as an example of Sting '[taking] on disguises in order to express indirectly parts of [his] identity that might be too threatening [or painful] to express directly'.[40] Is Sting engaging with the complex relationship with his father, but via the 'protection' of another persona? Is it this that enables the character Gideon to speak some honest home truths to his father comfortably at the end of the song, as it is not technically Sting speaking?

In addition to the lyrical content, the instrumental backing of this song can also be seen to accentuate the narrative, positioning it within a distinct social space almost like that of music in a film. For example, the slight increase in volume of the instrumental backing at 1:39 encourages Sting to sing louder, which has the effect of increasing the metaphorical size of the social space within which he is singing. This gradual increase in volume continues through to 2:20, which makes the sudden reduction in volume for the last few seconds of the track accentuate the character Gideon's now-quiet statement that regardless what his father says, he is not going to follow in his footsteps.

A fascinating aspect of Sting's recording of *The Last Ship* is that it is largely delivered in a Geordie accent – the accent that the young Gordon Sumner would have spoken in, but deliberately disguised during his years in the public eye. A recent review in *The Guardian* considered Sting's Geordie accent in *The Last Ship* to be a 'reasonable attempt at method acting'.[41] Although Sting could be seen to be taking on the persona of a north-eastern working-class male of the 1980s for this 'part', Sting seems to be addressing an aspect of his personality and identity that is more than simply 'acting', as it directly engages with his 'real person' alter ego, Gordon Sumner. While promoting the album with Sting, his friend Jimmy Nail refers to 'hear[ing] Gordon singing in his own dialect at times', with Sting responding by discussing how his 'funny voice' comes out when he is angry or drunk.[42] Perhaps it could be argued that it comes out when he is simply being himself.

In an interview for the *Sunday Times* in 1981, Sting commented on his escape from his northern England identity, stating,

I don't make a big thing out of being a Geordie. I've lost my accent, deliberately. We weren't a particularly happy family. It was the sort of family you inevitably go away from.[43]

Conducting an interview with Sting for *Time Out* magazine the following year in Newcastle, Chris Salewicz asserted that in 'his natural habitat, one sees Sting in a new light: suddenly his features appear extraordinarily Scandinavian'.[44] When Salewicz commented upon the 'unmistakable lilt' of his accent returning, Sting responded,

> My accent . . . is a consequence of having watched newscasters on TV and seeing where the real power in this country is. I think you do it as a strategy. My accent placed me exactly where I came from, in a terraced house on the dockside. And it wasn't to my advantage to let people know that at the time.[45]

Discussing the opportunities attending grammar school offered him, he continued,

> I started to visit kids from around here . . . So I made a decision: if that world was attractive to me, I wanted to be able to have it. I think it's always ruled my life – not materialism necessarily but the ability to make choices. Up until then I had no choices: you either worked down the pit, or you worked in the shipyard, or you were on the dole . . . So education, doing well at school, being an athlete, changing my accent, were all ways of giving me that option to leave Newcastle if I wanted to.[46]

All of this allows us to see that Sting's ongoing interface with Newcastle operates on a number of levels: superficially, simply by visiting the area, either privately or when on tour; through his lyrical content (about the shipyard and his parents in particular); through the use of northern musical signifiers (such as the Northumbrian pipes on numerous albums); or through the return/strategic use of his Geordie accent.[47] The latter is particularly apparent on albums such as *If on a Winter's Night . . .*, its associated DVD *A Winter's Night: Live from Durham Cathedral* (2009) and his more recent release *The Last Ship*, in which Sting re-engages with a number of themes he has explored in earlier work, such as his hometown of Wallsend, his complex relationship with his parents, his working-class background, the proximity of the Swan Hunter shipyard and the sea – all of which arguably cumulate to show him coming to terms with his 'northernness'.

Last Exit performing at the Imperial Hotel in Jesmond in 1975.

3 LAST EXIT

The post-Beatles era of the early 1970s was a time that witnessed the emergence of glam rock artists such as Marc Bolan and David Bowie; manufactured teeny bop stars such as Donny Osmond and the Bay City Rollers; and more serious adult music, with the middle-class, concept-driven subject matters of progressive rock bands such as Genesis and Emerson, Lake & Palmer beginning to make significant record sales. Although Sting was eventually compelled to a singles-based commercial imperative in his work with The Police, it was the literary subject matter of progressive rock, and in particular the musicianship associated with jazz rock, that was to inspire his early creativity and, most importantly, his determination to improve as a musician.

The Last Exit keyboard player Gerry Richardson is described in Sting's autobiography as a musician Sting was in awe of, having taught him the importance of daily practice, 'to read [music] better, [and] to be intrigued by the ever receding mystery of music . . . it was my friend Gerry who initiated and inspired me in these ideals.'[1] According to an article he wrote for Newcastle Libraries, Richardson met Sting in 1971 at the Northern Counties Teacher Training College, around 4 km (2½ miles) outside Newcastle city centre – and now part of Northumbria University.[2] After joining Richardson's band Earthrise, they pursued separate freelance careers in Newcastle between the years 1971 and 1974, prior to the formation of Last Exit:

I found myself playing seven nights a week in a different band in a South Shields night club while Sting started playing bass with a cabaret Trad Band (the Phoenix Jazzmen) and the Newcastle Big Band. He also played in the pit band at the University Theatre for a production of Joseph's Amazing Technicolor Dream Coat.[3]

Sting's first performances and recordings were not the norm for a musician who has progressed to such international commercial success. His first recording was, in fact, with the aforementioned Phoenix Jazzmen in 1973. Recorded at Impulse Sound Recording Studio in his hometown of Wallsend, its A-side is entitled 'I'm the King of the Swingers' and was made famous by Louis Prima in the Walt Disney cartoon *The Jungle Book* (1967), while the B-side was an adaptation of W. C. Handy's 'Beale Street Blues' (1916).[4] The Phoenix Jazzmen recording of the latter is a mid-tempo blues arrangement, featuring 'four in the bar' swing and periodic 'stop time' rhythm section. It is played in a style that can broadly be described as traditional jazz, and although the track is mainly a trumpet/vocal feature for Ronnie Young, with guitar (played by John Hedley) and clarinet solos, it does display Sting's early ability to play competent swing bass. The Phoenix Jazzmen arrangement of 'I'm the King of the Swingers' has a similar feel to the original recording by Louis Prima, although it moves between a 'jungle' beat in the verse to an uptempo swing for the choruses. As with the previous track, it features Ronnie Young on vocals – this time singing in a tone heavily influenced by Louis Armstrong. The line-up of both recordings features vocals, drums, guitar, bass, piano, clarinet, trombone and trumpet, and is clearly an attempt to duplicate the style of early jazz pioneers such as The Hot Fives, Joe Oliver and Jelly Roll Morton. Interestingly, John Hedley confirmed that the recording took place with the band surrounding a single microphone and the

louder instruments placed further away. This set-up was imple-
mented for practical reasons, and it is, in fact, a similar technique
to that used by the early jazz pioneers. The Phoenix Jazzmen in
many ways were an extension of the pre-rock-and-roll Dixieland
jazz revival of the 1950s, which took place in the UK with the likes
of Humphrey Lyttelton, Chris Barber, Kenny Ball and Acker Bilk,
inspiring numerous amateur bands to follow in their footsteps.
This early recording of 'I'm the King of the Swingers' was closely
followed by an album by the Newcastle Big Band, released in
1974.[5] Featuring jazz standard tracks, such as Cole Porter's 'Love
for Sale' and Charles Mingus's 'Better Get It in Your Soul',
alongside The Beatles' 'Hey Jude' and Jimmy Webb's 'MacArthur
Park', all eight of the tracks on the album were recorded live,
four of them at the Newcastle University Theatre Bar, and the
other half at The Pau Jazz Festival in France in the Municipal
Casino.[6] Although the recording may lack the 'tonal subtleties
and elegance of the original versions',[7] tracks such as 'Love for
Sale' have an inherent excitement, which gives the listener an
insight into the 'copious amounts of brown ale and lager' con-
sumed, and the 'ungodly fun [that was] had by all'.[8]

Andy Hudson started the Newcastle Big Band in 1968, and
Sting began to rehearse with the band in 1972 after an audition
upstairs at the Gosforth Hotel, a venue that was to play an important part in Sting's early musical development.[9] Although he was
not offered the gig initially because of his inability to sight-read
music at that point, Sting eventually got the job, playing regularly
for a Sunday morning residency at Newcastle University Theatre
Bar. He continued to play with the band up until he left the northeast of England for London towards the end of 1976. Reflecting on
the Big Band, Andy Hudson commented,

> The Big Band was a concoction of musicians, who happened
> to be available on a Sunday lunchtime . . . the rhythm section

Photo shoot of Newcastle Big band, featuring Sting (back row, third from left) at Newcastle Guildhall.

became Last Exit. The Big Band performed virtually every Sunday for about three or four years. It started as a university band . . . and I was probably the worst musician but the best organiser. So I put it all together.[10]

Hudson also discussed how, for Sting's fiftieth birthday, he forwarded him some old accounts he had found. He continued,

We used to split the money up on the door and it was split in a certain way. I got more because I was there longer – I had to take and set the sound system up. The arrangers . . . they used to get a bit more because they did the arrangements. Sting

A.J. HUDSON	44	5 -	4 -	✓
J. PEARCE	4	4 -	3 -	
N. STANGER :	46	4 -	3 -	
D. EDDY	24.60	3 -	2 -	
G. SUMNER	30.50	2 -	2 -	
K. HENLY	31.50	2 -	2 -	
J. HEDLEY				
G. SHEPPARD	25	2 -	2 -	
A. LOANE	24.50	2 -	2 -	
L. WEYMES	4	—	2 -	
C. CARMICHAEL	30	2 -	2 -	
G. HEDLEY	20.50	2 -	2 -	
S. LANGDON	23	2 -	2 -	
L. LIDDEL	22.50	2 ✓	2 -	
G. SOLOMON	22	2 -	2 -	
M. WALSH	22	2 -	2 -	
B. CHESTER	18	2 -	2 -	
R. McLEAN	21	2 ✓	1 -	
OTHERS }				
A. PARKER	26	—	2 -	
R. CARR	24.50	3 -	2 -	
A. BERTORELLI	26 -	2 -	2 -	
P. VOLPE	26	2 -	2 -	
R. TIPADY	18	2 ✓	1 -	
C. AITCHISON	22	2 ✓	1 -	↗

Newcastle Big Band 1973

Newcastle Big Band accounts from 1973, including Gordon Sumner's salary.

occasionally used to get more than everybody else because he used to carry stuff around.[11]

Regarding Sting's audition with the big band in 1972, Hudson confirmed Sting's account in his autobiography, in which he recounts originally not passing the audition:

> we found one week we did not have a bass player. Sting asked if he could have a go, and I said yes. He came up, and he really wasn't very good, he would be the first to admit it . . . I liked his whole approach, so I said to him look, take the music home, flog it to death and learn it – and he did. When he came back the following week and the week after he was fine.[12]

Like Gerry Richardson, John Hedley is still in contact with Sting, and has been one of the most established guitarists on the northeast of England music scene for over forty years. A few years Sting's senior, and described as his 'mentor' in Sting's autobiography, Hedley originally moved from Newcastle to London in 1966, moving back to the northeast in 1972.[13] Upon his return, he was invited to audition for local traditional jazz band the Phoenix Jazzmen the same year. The band at that point had a residency at the now-demolished Blue Star Pub, across the road from St James' Park, the home of Newcastle United Football Ground – Sting's local club which he still supports. Although the Phoenix Jazzmen preferably wanted a banjo player, Hedley was accepted on guitar. It was at this audition that he met bass player Gordon Sumner. According to Hedley, Sting had seen him in 1971, performing with the London-based band Every Which Way (which featured Brian Davidson of The Nice) at Newcastle City Hall, so was already aware of who he was when they met.[14]

Hedley described how Sting used to come to visit his flat in Newcastle while he was attending Northern Counties Teacher Training College in 1972, while training to be a schoolteacher. He commented, 'he used to spend Saturdays with me, just reading [music notation] stuff . . . he had never heard of [jazz rock] musicians such as John McLaughlin, Chick Corea, or any of that.'[15] During their regular conversations, Hedley distinctly remembers Sting outlining his ambitions to be a jazz musician: 'I am going to learn to sing like Cleo Lane and play the bass like Stanley Clarke.'[16] According to Hedley, Sting did not appear to be interested in rock music at this point – bands such as Led Zeppelin were on the periphery of his musical horizons. If this is the case, it is apparent that his musical tastes had 'matured' in the years after leaving school, as Sting recounts visiting the now demolished Club A'GoGo in Percy Street, Newcastle, on a number of occasions. His first visit was in 1966, aged fifteen, to see the Graham Bond Organisation (featuring Jack Bruce and Ginger Baker), followed by John Mayall's Bluesbreakers the following year. In December 1967 Sting was also present at the club to see The Jimi Hendrix Experience, an event he describes as resulting in his 'world view [being] significantly altered' in his autobiography.[17]

It is also apparent, from reading Sting's autobiography and the recollections of his 'best mate' James Berryman, that he was, like many people of his generation, a Beatles and Rolling Stones fan. Indeed, according to Berryman, Sting attempted to see The Beatles on 4 December 1965 at Newcastle City Hall, but was unable to get a ticket.[18]

John Hedley recalled Sting's ability to play complex bass lines while singing vocals simultaneously, often across the beat – a skill that was particularly noticeable during his years with The Police. Hedley recounted a conversation he had with Sting regarding his practice of humorously 'mirroring' the solos of a member of the Phoenix Jazzmen in the early 1970s – Ronnie Young:

Ronnie played the same solo every night, and Sting, being
aware of this, used to scat sing his solo 'note for note'.
Ronnie's hero was a guy called Nat Gonella (1918–1998). Now
Nat Gonella had been around in the '30s, '40s and '50s in the
Midlands and the South [of England], he played trumpet and
sang. His big hero was Louis Armstrong. So what he [Ronnie
Young] had done was . . . he had learnt the Louis Armstrong
solos. So you have got Nat Gonella who had copied all the
solos from Louis Armstrong. Then you have got Ronnie
Young who has copied them from Nat Gonella. So he [Sting]
is singing Louis Armstrong once removed.[19]

Although Sting alludes to this event in his biography, he does not
discuss its impact on his early musical development. In addition
to his time with Last Exit, these experiences were surely foundational, not only during his tenure with The Police, but for his early
solo career, which was so heavily influenced by jazz.

On the subject of jazz, alongside a number of other unknown
European bands such as Metropolitan Jazz Prague, Barrelhouse
Jazzband (from Germany) and Szabados Quartet (from France),
Last Exit travelled to Spain for what they thought would be a
five-day event to perform as part of the fringe programme of
the San Sebastian Jazz Festival (which took place 19–24 July 1975),
performing in the town square of the old city at the Plaza de
la Trinidad on 23 July. That year, the headliners of the festival
included Ella Fitzgerald, Oscar Peterson and Dizzy Gillespie, big-
name jazz stars who would have been touring Europe at the time.
John Hedley confirmed that Last Exit were positioned within the
amateur section of the festival, which was essentially a competition – 'whoever won the heat went to the final on the Saturday.'[20]
Last Exit obviously performed well, as they won the competition,
gaining not only a place in the final on Saturday 26 July, but by
default 'another week in nearby Bilbao'.[21]

programa del festival

X FESTIVAL DE JAZZ DE SAN SEBASTIAN
19 al 24 de julio

DIA 19

19,30 horas: FESTIVAL DE JAZZ PROFESIONAL
(Plaza de la Trinidad)
GUY LAFITTE
ANDRE «PEPE» PERSIANY
ROLLAND LOBLIGEOIS
ROGER PARABOSCHI
OLIVER JACKSON

23,00 horas FESTIVAL DE JAZZ PROFESIONAL
(Plaza de la Trinidad)
ILLINOIS JACQUET
JOHN HARDEE
GENE «Mighty flea» CONNORS
GEORGE DUVIVIER
JOHNNY GUARNIERI
OLIVER JACKSON

DIA 20

21,00 horas: FESTIVAL DE JAZZ PROFESIONAL
(Palacio Municipal de Deportes)
TETE MONTOLIU Y CONJUNTO (Eric Peters y Peer Wyboris)
ELLA FITZGERALD

DIA 21

12,00 horas: PROYECCION DE PELICULAS
(Sala de Cultura de la Caja de Ahorros Municipal)
17,30 horas: FESTIVAL DE JAZZ AMATEUR
(Plaza de la Trinidad)
PHOENIX JAZZBAND (Inglaterra) Tradicional
ATO (España) Moderno
DIZZY BATS SEPTET (Suiza) Jazz Pop
21,00 horas: FESTIVAL DE JAZZ PROFESIONAL
(Palacio Municipal de Deportes)
OSCAR PETERSON
DIZZY GILLESPIE
(Alexander Gafa, Earl C. May, Granville W. Roker)
01,30 horas: JAM SESSION (Bajos del Ayuntamiento)

DIA 22

12,00 y 17,00 horas: PROYECCION DE PELICULAS
(Sala de Cultura de la Caja de Ahorros Municipal)

19,30 horas: FESTIVAL DE JAZZ AMATEUR
(Plaza de la Trinidad)
ELAOIN EXTRAPOLATION (Suiza) Jazz Rock
BRASSY BREW (Alemania) Jazz Pop
HOT LIPS (Dinamarca) Tradicional
METROPOLITAN JAZZ PRAGUE (Checoslovaquia) Tradicional
23,00 horas: FESTIVAL DE JAZZ PROFESIONAL
(Plaza de la Trinidad)
THE BARRELHOUSE JAZZBAND & ANGI DOMDEY
TREVOR RICHARDS NEW ORLEANS TRIO
DUO GLADKOWSKI-ZGRAJA
01,30 horas: JAM SESSION (Bajos del Ayuntamiento)

DIA 23

12,00 y 17,00 horas: PROYECCION DE PELICULAS
(Sala de Cultura de la Caja de Ahorros Municipal)
19,30 horas: FESTIVAL DE JAZZ AMATEUR
(Plaza de la Trinidad)
SCANIAZZ (Suecia) Tradicional
FOKAMACASE (Francia) Moderno
LAST EXIT (Inglaterra) Jazz Rock
SZABADOS QUARTET (Hungría) Free
23,00 horas: FESTIVAL DE JAZZ PROFESIONAL
(Plaza de la Trinidad)
JOE «Mighty» YOUNG y cuarteto
REVERENDO CLEOPHUS ROBINSON y Trio,
Napoleon Brown, Junior y Paul Robinson
MARION WILLIAMS
01,30 horas: JAM SESSION (Bajos del Ayuntamiento)

DIA 24

12,00 y 17,00 horas: PROYECCION DE PELICULAS
(Sala de Cultura de la Caja de Ahorros Municipal)
19,30 horas: FESTIVAL DE JAZZ PROFESIONAL
(Plaza de la Trinidad)
DOROTHY DONEGAN
JACKY BYARD
RAY BRYANT
JO JONES
23,00 horas: FESTIVAL DE JAZZ PROFESIONAL
(Plaza de la Trinidad)
HARRY «Sweet» EDISON
EARL WARREN
TEDDY WILSON
MAJOR HOLLEY
PANAMA FRANCIS

Este programa podrá ser alterado sin que quepa responsabilidad alguna a la Organización por ello.

Caja de Ahorros Municipal de San Sebastian
CAM

Programme of the 1975 San Sebastian Jazz Festival, with Last Exit performing on 23 July.

These activities took place while Sting was a full-time school-teacher using his summer holiday to pursue his ambitions to be a professional musician. During this time, between the summer of 1974 and December 1976, in addition to his jazz gigs with Last Exit and the Newcastle Big Band, Sting also performed in working men's clubs as a bass player in and around the area. The skill base expected of Sting at this time would have included the ability to sight-read notated music and knowledge of a large repertoire of cover songs, all of which could be played in any style. This work is not high profile – the musicians and bands are usually considered secondary to bingo, what Sting described as a 'quasi-religious ritual', which was/is given great importance in many working men's clubs in the region.[22] One of the great ironies that Sting would have discovered is that some of the musicians he was performing with were already experienced professionals, who would have found themselves serendipitously thrown in with newcomers such as himself.

> To gig night after night had an honourable and romantic tradition, at least it appeared so to us . . . if you can play well and are versatile enough, you might be able to join that illustrious brotherhood, that select band of musicians, who provide the backing behind crooners, jugglers, strippers, magicians and singing comedians. To be a professional musician, a journeyman able to sight-read sufficiently to hold down a job, to play whatever style was required – this was the ultimate goal.[23]

In this gigging environment, the 'band leaders' Sting worked with, who would have taken a greater share of the income, would have been responsible for choosing songs, finding the right musicians, generally fronting the evening and finding work. Sting would have been expected to travel, sometimes large distances, in addition to working unsociable hours regularly on weekends and public holidays like Christmas and New Year's Eve. These are all skills/traits that Sting would later adopt when he moved to London and forged a career with The Police. The vast majority of the music performed in these bands would be cover versions – original music was totally out of the question in working men's clubs. As confirmed by Gerry Richardson, even Last Exit, who were considered to be a band that played 'original material', played many cover versions as part of their repertoire, in order to keep audiences at their residences interested.

Both in the lead-up to the formation of Last Exit and during
its lifespan, Sting also performed in a few musical theatre productions. His first job was in the pit orchestra in a ten-week season
of Andrew Lloyd Webber and Tim Rice's *Joseph and the Amazing
Technicolor Dreamcoat* at the Newcastle University Theatre commencing on 6 June 1974, which, according to a recent article, Sting
regarded as his 'first professional job as a musician'.[24] The experience prompted Sting later to state that he had fallen 'in love with
the magic of the theatre and become intoxicated by its tawdry
glamour and cheap illusion, its noise and its pretence'.[25] This
was followed by a Tony Hatch-penned play entitled *Rock Nativity*
from 18 December 1974 to 25 January 1975, another quasi-religious
show commencing in December 1975 entitled *Hellfire* (both of
which were also staged at Newcastle University Theatre) and
other shows in which Last Exit acted as the backing band.[26] In the
article, Sting places these early experiences in the lineage of *The
Last Ship* – which at the time of writing had recently completed a
short, ill-fated season on Broadway.

> I began my professional life in the theatre, never imagining
> that I would ever attempt to write something or ever end up
> on a stage in one of them. I was happy in the pit. I was very
> proud of my 60 quid a week.[27]

Towards the end of the summer of 1974, Sting was offered a
position as a schoolteacher – at St Paul's First School in nearby
Cramlington. Although he never intended on making it an
ongoing career, financial necessity forced him to accept the job,
starting in September 1974. In doing so, Sting made the day job
compromise that so many musicians often have to make – not
only at the start of their careers, but often throughout it. These
compromises can range from the musical (that is, playing in
the orchestra pit on a music theatre production or having to

perform in function / cover bands), to working outside the profession in a 'parallel' career. As Sting reminisced, this multi-tasking role required dedication:

> I drive back up the A1 to [the] Gosforth [Hotel], then carry the gear up the stairs, set it up, and return home to pick up my bass amp and speaker cabinet and make another journey north . . . we have to do the same thing in reverse after playing and singing for two hours.[28]

Last Exit were officially formed in October 1974, taking their name from Hubert Selby's cult book based in lower-class Brooklyn – *Last Exit from Brooklyn* (1964).[29] Guitarist John Hedley elaborated Sting's depiction during an interview and proceeded to confirm that the band's first rehearsal was indeed on Friday 4 October 1974 at the Coach Lane Campus of Northern Counties Teacher Training College, where Sting was a student. This was closely followed by their inaugural gig at the Gosforth Hotel on Wednesday 16 October 1974, for which he was paid the princely sum of £1.70. After a gig at Newcastle University on Friday 18 October, the band performed at the Gosforth Hotel another two times in October alone – on Wednesday 23 October and a week later on Wednesday 30 October. This venue obviously has great significance for Sting, who performed there regularly over a two-year period – the venue is mentioned throughout his autobiography and was also included as part of a backdrop of 'slideshow' images during performances of *The Last Ship* at the Sage in Gateshead between 24 and 25 April 2015. The London-born journalist Phil Sutcliffe, who started in 1969 as a graduate apprentice with the Newcastle-based *Evening Chronicle*, remembered the Gosforth Hotel always being at capacity (seventy to one hundred people). Last Exit provided the backdrop to his new life as a music journalist in 1974, the year that they were formed:

at that moment they were my favourite band in the world'.
you had your back to the windows that were on the street,
and the band are facing the window, and so you're looking
at the band against the wall there – all rammed in around
tables . . . always full, great atmosphere.[30]

In a conversation with the author, Newcastle-based music journalist Sid Smith, who attended the vast majority of Last Exit's
performances at the Gosforth Hotel, explained that he believed
that the band regarded themselves primarily as a 'jazz group
that did songs', with a set that was comprised of 'hard core jazz
rock . . . melodic East Coast influenced music . . . bossa nova,
covers and comedy numbers – it was all round entertainment'.[31]
Gerry Richardson described Last Exit as 'an eclectic band', with
a repertoire that included 'funk, blues, folk, reggae, rock 'n' roll,
soul, jazz rock, jazz funk, prog rock, you name it, we played it'.[32]
This allowed the band to be able to develop a good reputation as
a live band – but 'really the kiss of death commercially'. Gerry
Richardson continued,

> One minute we sounded like Yes, the next Tower of Power,
> and the next Shakin' Stevens and the Sunsets. I can't believe
> how naive we were. We thought we would be rewarded for
> our versatility not realising that record companies wanted
> bands with a defined image that was easy to market.[33]

Asked about the reasons behind the breadth of material Last Exit
had developed, Richardson responded,

> I reckon when the band fell to bits, we had a repertoire of
> 60–70 tunes . . . It was just the thing of having two residencies.
> We were on every Wednesday night at the Gosforth Hotel for
> about two years, and we were on every third Sunday at the

[Newcastle] University Theatre – so you couldn't keep playing the same stuff. We played an enormous number of covers
as well.[34]

Discussing the repertoire of Last Exit, Phil Sutcliffe commented,

That's why they could play residencies and draw the same
crowd every week, because they would play a hugely different
set every week . . . and so you saw the band you loved . . . with
different songs, and so it was endlessly enjoyable and satisfy-
ing to go and see Last Exit week after week. I expect that was
common back then and why bands could play residencies.[35]

Sting reiterated Richardson's point regarding the difference
between a jobbing live band and the requirements of a record
label when remembering a later Last Exit recording session at
Pathway Studios in Islington, London:

we want to demonstrate just how versatile we are. If we had
been more experienced, we would have realized that versatility is not something the record industry values at all. What
they are looking for is something singular and fresh. We don't
yet understand that versatility is a premium for nightclub
bands and journeyman musicians, not pop acts.[36]

Sid Smith recalled Last Exit playing 'classic jazz' albums before,
after and during the intervals at the Gosforth Hotel, a phenomenon that he believed 'was a way of reinforcing that [jazz]
connection with the punters – many of whom wouldn't have had
any idea about jazz'.[37] Although there were few jazz-rock bands
working in the northeast of England at the time, the area had a
heritage of both jazz and rock genres – musicians such as John
McLaughlin lived in Whitley Bay during the 1950s and recorded a

live album with the EmCee Five in 1967 at the New Orleans Club on Newcastle's Forth Banks.[38] Living just around the corner from the Gosforth Hotel, Smith recalled his first experience of the venue – and Last Exit's surprising popularity and quality:

> Having entered the side door which led upstairs . . . the first thing that I noticed was that there was a queue . . . Any night of the week there were ten or twelve pubs with bands on [in Newcastle], you never wanted for seeing a band. The thing was there was never usually a huge queue.[39]

Regarding that first performance, he continued,

> What was different about Last Exit was that there was a demeanor about them. It wasn't cocky, it wasn't swaggering, but it was instantly professional . . . Right from the second they started playing they were right on form.[40]

Smith recalls drummer Ronnie Pearson doing the talking between songs at the start, but noticed the emergence of Sting gradually taking over this lead role as the months progressed.

> Over time, as the band gathered momentum, and developed a kind of an image, front and centre of that image . . . was Sting. Who else are you going to put at the front of the band?[41]

Examination of a bootleg recorded at the Gosforth Hotel in 1976 bears testimony to some of these accounts, with Sting having a very informal, at times 'humorously abusive', relationship with the audience – the type of relationship which is not possible in larger venues. Listening to the recording, despite its poor sound quality, it is apparent that the band are very well rehearsed, with many of the songs being used to feature the instrumental prowess of the players. The audience are obviously familiar with the material and, most importantly, Sting is very much depicted as the leader in this recording, not only introducing songs, having banter with the audience and introducing the band, but energetically counting songs in when required. Commenting on the ways in which she assisted Sting with his stagecraft during these years, his wife at the time, Frances Tomelty, commented,

> When I first saw Last Exit he [Sting] used to look around a lot. He thought he was drawing the audience in, but I knew it defused concentration and made him look nervy and awkward. I said 'be still'. He was and it worked. These days he doesn't look at you, you look at him.[42]

Gerry Richardson outlined how Newcastle Big Band leader and Newcastle Festival director Andy Hudson managed to secure two weekly residences: 'one at the Gosforth Hotel on a Wednesday night and a bit later on, every third Sunday lunchtime in the University Theatre Bar [shared with the Newcastle Big Band and another local Jazz Rock Band – The Steve Brown Band]'.[43] Commencing in October 1975, Sting had already been performing at this venue for around three years with the Newcastle Big Band and on a less formal basis with Last Exit.

Jeffrey the Barak played drums in The Steve Brown Band, who – having emerged a few years prior to Last Exit – were more established, offering the band support slots, both in Newcastle and later in London. Describing their relationship as 'rivals, but kinda friendly', he remembered both sitting in with Last Exit when drummer Ronnie Pearson was 'at the bar', and also helping Sting and his bandmates carry their equipment up and down the stairs of the Gosforth Hotel. Regarding the Last Exit support slots, he commented,

The Gosforth Hotel today.

> They were always opening for us. We played this gig at
> Newcastle University Theatre [Bar]. They were on first and
> they were very good – they got encores. By the time we came
> on it was kinda late. So halfway through the first number
> there was this mass exodus – 'cause all these people had to
> catch the last bus [Laughs].[44]

A larger venue than the Gosforth Hotel, the Newcastle University
Theatre Bar was a place at which Sting performed regularly with
both Last Exit and the Newcastle Big Band – and also occasionally
as part of a trio during the interval, when major jazz artists were
performing at the adjacent Newcastle University Theatre. After
Sting had left for London and formed The Police, he and Last
Exit performed a 'reunion concert' at the venue one last time in
December 1977. Barak was present at this event and recalled how
Sting had progressed:

I remember some very big differences. Sting had moved on – a lot. He was a better bass player, better singer and a better performer – he had a lot more stage presence. And he looked world famous. He had his green army parachute suit, he was moving like he did in The Police. He kinda overshadowed Ronnie and Gerry and the other guys . . . It was like seeing a world-class gig back at the University Theatre [Bar] . . . He didn't try and dominate, but you could see it was somebody very special on stage.[45]

Sid Smith, who was also at the performance, recalled,

He certainly had his hair changed . . . There was definitely a sense that this was not old Sting, this was new Sting. This was a re-sharpened, re-tooled, altogether more focused and pointed, heat seeking . . . He always did move good, he always did look good – this was just on steroids.[46]

Asked about Last Exit's musical influences, keyboard player Gerry Richardson cites jazz-rock bands such as The Crusaders, Tower of Power, The Mahavishnu Orchestra, Chick Corea and Herbie Hancock as their main inspiration, but confirms that Sting was also interested in folk-influenced music such as Fairport Convention and James Taylor at that point. Once these residencies became established, they eventually resulted in the band supporting established acts at Newcastle University Theatre and the local Polytechnic. Although Richardson remembers Osibisa and Ian Carr's Nucleus specifically, Sting recounts supporting Jon Hiseman's Colosseum in Redcar and Alan Price at Newcastle City Hall in the autumn of 1976.[47] The band had also previously performed a concert at Newcastle City Hall on 26 October 1975, in which they supported 'The Orchestral Tubular Bells', conducted by David Bedford. Performed by the

Northern Concert Orchestra, this concert actually featured Andy Summers on guitar, and was therefore the first time Sting and Summers performed together in the same space, although with different ensembles. An audience member remembers the gig not being well attended, Last Exit having played in the interval between the two movements of Tubular Bells.[48] This is confirmed by Andy Summers:

> There is an intermission spot that will be filled by a local band called Last Exit, a jazz fusion group. They have a bass player named Sting and are supposed to be quite good, so I decide to watch them. I stand at the back of the hall and watch for about five minutes and then wander off for a cheese roll and a cup of tea.[49]

In the concert programme, Last Exit are said to be playing 'their first concert hall appearance', mixing 'electric jazz and jazz-rock', including 'their own material' and 'repertoire of other peoples [sic]'. They are also reported to play frequently at Blakey Ridge – 'once the home of Back Door'.[50] Andy Summers actually gets a specific mention in the programme, which outlines how 'the most effective guitarists are always the ones who appreciate economy'. After mentioning his time at San Fernando State University studying music theory and classical guitar, he is reported to have been playing in Kevin Coyne's band, his time spent working with Zoot Money, Soft Machine and Eric Burdon.

Although there is no record of Last Exit's set list, it is interesting to speculate that Summers that night would have been highly likely to have heard early incarnations of some of the songs which would not only change Sting's life, but his own, assisting him in the progression from being a jobbing musician approaching middle age to a member of one of the most successful groups in the history of popular music.

Newcastle City Hall.

Towards the end of 1975, John Hedley decided to leave Last Exit, and was replaced by Terry Ellis.[51] At this point, Hedley was becoming increasingly disillusioned with the musical direction of the band and recollected that prior to the demos recorded at Impulse 'none of them [other members of the band] had been to London [in fact] none of them had been to a recording studio before.'[52] Hedley, who had been a professional musician since 1969, reflected upon his reason for leaving the band:

> They want[ed] to go to London and make it, and I say look, with this band you won't. At the time, the bloody Sex Pistols were kicking in . . . I said they will laugh you out of town man.[53]

ORCHESTRAL
TUBULAR BELLS

Northern Concert Orchestra
conducted by David Bedford
solo guitar: Andy Summers

plus
Last Exit

Newcastle City Hall   26th October

Programme cover of Tubular Bells concert: Newcastle City Hall, 26 October 1975.

Having decided they were going to get some gigs in London,
Hedley remembers a proposed performance at Dingwalls (in
Camden, London), where, as opposed to getting paid (in the trad-
itional sense), '[the band] had to contribute toward the hire of the
PA, so they were paying for van hire, petrol, and an arm and a leg
to appear . . . I decided, I am out of here man.'[54]

An article by Phil Sutcliffe (then of *Sounds* magazine), dated 8
January 1977, covers the personal and financial sacrifices Last Exit
faced, when attempting to bridge the 480 km (300 miles) between
Newcastle and London.[55] Starting with the loading of the equipment into the van in Newcastle and then continuing with the
long journey to London for the slot at Dingwalls supporting Isaac
Guillory, the article tracks the hard realities of a band who are
reported to be a 'big fish in a small pool'. The gig was, in fact, the
start of an extended visit to London in September 1976, which also

included recording some demos at Pathway Studios in Islington – the very place that The Police were to record their debut single, 'Fall Out'.

Discussing the *Sounds* article and the journey from Newcastle to London, Phil Sutcliffe stated,

> The only way I was able to sell a piece on Last Exit was to make it part of a theme like that. Of course it was all about Last Exit, but to the editor I was going to travel with a band from the provinces, to the great mecca of London, and they were going to play a trial gig . . . and see how it went . . . You could tell the hard work of that day, you loaded up the van, and you would go on this enormous drive as it was then, in a heavily laden Transit. You're jammed in with all of your equipment . . . you're making your first leap. It's a big adventure, there's a showcase . . . well that means a lot to you if you're the guys doing it you know. You're gonna play this venue, which is not massive, but is very well known . . . this is their chance of the breakthrough.[56]

An article in Newcastle's *Evening Chronicle* in March 1975 reflected this north–south divide, the music scene in Newcastle at the time of Last Exit being described as suffering from a 'terrible apathy', with 'many promising young bands turning their backs on Tyneside and heading south'.[57] The reason for this phenomenon is described by local artist Steve Brown, leader of the Steve Brown Band:

> This area does not deserve all the greats who have come from up here. It is not like the South – all the clubs are closing down and there is hardly anywhere left to play fairly frequently . . . You can practise all you like but if you don't get the shows it is no earthly use.[58]

As The Steve Brown Band do, Last Exit provide an interesting snapshot of a Newcastle-based band, who attempted to follow in the commercial success of other northern icons such as The Shadows, The Animals, Brian Ferry, Geordie and Lindisfarne, in addition to the musical footsteps of one of their major influences – Warner Brothers-signed Back Door. It is apparent that Back Door provided an interesting archetype for Last Exit. First, although far more avant-garde (having a clear influence of Ornette Coleman and Archie Shepp – on their first album in particular), they were a northern-England-based jazz-fusion group, detached from London, who were centred around a bass player (Colin Hodgkinson), who was also a vocalist. Like Last Exit, their early recordings were self-produced on a shoestring budget, recording their first album (*Back Door*, 1971) on a portable Ampex four-track recorder – with the intention of selling it at gigs.[59] Although originally rejected by record companies because of their lack of vocals (and lack of commercial potential), they eventually obtained a record deal with Warner Brothers. As Last Exit had, the band built their audience at a local venue, the Lion Inn in North Yorkshire, which featured on the cover of their debut release. Unlike Last Exit, Back Door eventually progressed beyond their local status, touring America with Emerson, Lake & Palmer, in addition to releasing two more subsequent albums (not with the original line-up) prior to splitting up in 1977. Although there is little musical resemblance between Back Door and Last Exit, the bass player Colin Hodgkinson's style obviously had an impact on Sting. It is also possible to propose that their three piece, bass-dominated line-up may have informed Sting on some level when forming The Police.

Sting's duties in Last Exit became more profound over time, gradually taking over the dominant role as composer and vocalist, so his time with this band has to be regarded as an important

training ground, both musically and in terms of developing his
stagecraft. Although very firmly a jazz-rock ensemble, Last Exit's
music did contain some progressive influences, such as tuneful
melodies, instrumental proficiency and complex time signatures,
in addition to following in the footsteps of ensembles such as Soft
Machine, Steely Dan and The Doors by having a name inspired by
literature. Sid Smith, reflecting on Last Exit concerts at both the
Gosforth Hotel and Newcastle University Theatre, summarizes
the band's and Sting's ascendancy:

> you just knew it wasn't a question of 'if' but rather 'when' they
> were going to get signed. There was that heady expectation
> when the band was in full flight; whether they were blasting
> through a cracking version of Hymn Of The Seventh Galaxy,
> an irresistibly catchy original number (even the daft one called
> The Grand Hotel) or a samba-smooth take on Stevie Wonder's
> Creepin'. There was a dead certainty that this time, the Gods
> would smile; this time musical skill would win out and the
> world would be converted to the cause. And then when the
> packed house chin-wagged during the interval, what it boiled
> down to was the realisation that it was just one member of the
> band who was going to fly high. It felt a bit disloyal to admit
> it; after all, Ronnie was a great drummer, Gerry was a demon
> when the Hammond got cranked up and John (or his replace-
> ment, Terry) did a top-notch job on the guitar. Yet it couldn't
> be ducked, singer and bassist, Sting was the one who had what
> the tabloids would call 'star quality.' Sting just had that 'some-
> thing else' about him.[60]

The 'something else' that Smith refers to during his time in
Newcastle is now largely restricted to the annals of middle-aged
memory, although there are a few recorded remnants. In addition

Poster of Last Exit supporting the Steve Brown Band at Newcastle University Theatre in 1975.

to the odd audience bootleg, Sting recorded early versions of some of his well-known songs during his time in Newcastle, a small independent studio in Wallsend having a particularly important resonance with his past and future.

4 EARLY RECORDINGS

During the 1960s, when popular music was developing from its rhythm and blues roots to the technological experimentation highlighted on albums such as *Sgt. Pepper's Lonely Hearts Club Band* (1967), the place of the recording studio was to become more prominent in the minds of both musicians and audiences – Abbey Road (in St John's Wood, London) and Electric Lady Studios (in Greenwich Village, New York) are two examples. Also building on the tradition of small studios that emerged during the 1950s such as Sam Philips's Sun Studios and Norman Petty's Clovis, a number of independent studios began to emerge in the UK, most famously Joe Meek's studio, which opened in the early '60s in a three-storey flat at 30 Holloway Road in Islington.

Sting's early songs were largely recorded at Impulse Sound Recording Studio, in Wallsend. Founded by David Wood in 1967, the studio was arguably the first commercial progressive recording studio in the Newcastle region. Wood, who met Sting in 1972 during his tenure with the Newcastle Big Band, set the studio up after accepting a £250 redundancy payment from local company Procter & Gamble. Undertaking his new role as 'full-time professional' from the start, Wood was responsible for recording the original demos of Lindisfarne songs such as 'Meet Me on the Corner' and 'Fog on the Tyne' at Impulse. According to Wood, many of Joan Armatrading's original demo recordings were also recorded at the studio, when she was working in the chorus of

Hair at the Theatre Royal in Newcastle during the late 1960s. In addition to his recording activities, Wood also started a number of other independent record labels in order to diversify income, including the folk-based Rubber Records (which recorded artists such as Mike Harding, Five Hand Reel and The Krankies) and Wudwink for jazz. It was with this latter label that Last Exit were to record their only single, 'Whispering Voices', penned by keyboard player Gerry Richardson. In later years, Wood formulated Neat Records – which was responsible for output from bands such as Raven and Venom – as part of the 'new wave of British heavy metal'. The studio remained in existence for around 36 years, closing in 2002.

Only a short walk from where Sting grew up, Impulse Sound Recording Studio was situated over three floors within the old Gaumont Cinema complex (originally the Borough Theatre) – coincidentally above the boarded-up Mr Braidford's Music Shop, which Sting frequently visited as a child. The Borough Theatre opened as a live music venue in 1909 and, after being taken over by the Gaumont corporation in 1928, was developed into a bingo hall in 1960. It was subsequently used for a number of purposes (including Impulse Sound Recording Studio), prior to being demolished in March 2011. The site currently houses private apartments.

According to Wood, when the studio first started, the space was still being used as a bingo hall and amusement arcade, the studio space originally occupying the dressing room area on the first of the three floors.

> The first floor was a kind of reception area and small mono two-track studio – which was initially extended to another studio further in – before being closed down.[1]

Another studio was consequently built on the top floor, which, according to Wood, 'was a bit of a nuisance as you had to climb

Site of the Borough Theatre, the Old Gaumont Cinema and later Impulse Sound Recording Studio.

four flights of stairs . . . there was no lift.' Sting was to record on an eight-track Ampex recorder in this space, although the Studio did progress to sixteen track, and eventually to 24-track in later years.

Mickey Sweeney, who was responsible for installing the mixing desk that Last Exit recorded on, described the Live Room of the studio as being generally a 'dead space', a factor which forced him to record brass bands on the staircase in order to get additional ambience. Sweeney remembers the studio having a ten-channel mixer into the eight-track machine – facilitating the use of up to ten microphones at any one time. He also recounted how 'the bones of the [Last Exit] songs were recorded in a [single] live take, with 4 mics being used on the drum kit, with the bass and keys usually being direct injected (into the mixing desk).'[2] The recordings were made using a guide vocal, with any additional parts and final vocals added afterwards as overdubs. Although he had no precise details, Sweeney remembered the original eight-track desk being purchased by a recording studio in the Netherlands when Impulse sold it.

Regarding the control room of the studio during Sting's time, Sweeney described it as being around 12 m × 6 m (40 ft × 20 ft) and 'really odd shaped . . . with the desk unusually facing away from the studio window, forcing the engineer/producer to turn around to see the musicians in the live space'.[3] The studio was

> built around a stone staircase that went up . . . occupying the corner of the building. All the rooms on the west side were tiny, while the other side was bigger . . . almost going to a point.[4]

Sweeney remembers being able to

> open the slides in one of the rooms upstairs and look down, as if you were looking down from the top of the curtains . . . it just dropped down into nothingness, and you could hear the bingo caller if you opened the big steel door.[5]

All the rooms upstairs had been dressing rooms and offices from the days of the music hall, and it was in these spaces, when reappropriated as a recording studio, that Sting would make his early demos.

All of the Last Exit recording sessions were engineered by Sweeney, who secured the job in 1972 after an extended tenure working as a live sound engineer with Lindisfarne. After the original line-up of the band split up in 1973, he progressed to co-produce Alan Hull's solo album *Pipedream* (1973) at Trident Studios in London, in conjunction with producer Roy Thomas

Baker – who went on to work on Queen's 'Bohemian Rhapsody' (1975). He left Impulse in 1980 for artistic reasons, preferring to focus on folk-influenced music, as opposed to the new wave of British heavy metal that was becoming popular at the time. On meeting Sting for the first time in 1972, Sweeney recalled thinking of him as 'an Adonis, as soon as he walked into the room with the band, I thought my God, this guy is going to

Mickey Sweeney in the control room of Impulse during the time Sting used it.

go somewhere – I just knew it.'[6] Although he described Sting
as having 'charisma and great talent', he considered Sting's
vocals to be 'still in development', as he was still 'singing from
his throat'.[7] According to Gerry Richardson, 'Ronnie [Pearson]
used to do quite a bit of singing [at the start]', with Last Exit
'gradually becoming more and more Sting's band' over time.[8]
It appears that Sting's vocal capabilities, songwriting and leadership qualities developed hand in hand in those early years.
Sweeney remembers recording the band on his own, with an
inexperienced Sting being very much led (as opposed to being a
leader) at that point, one of his more lucid memories being of
Sting asking him for a cassette at the end of one of the recording
sessions, without allowing time for it to be prepared.

Asked about the logistics of Last Exit's recordings at Impulse,
John Hedley discussed how David Wood used to fit the band
around paying customers – relating that

> he used to ring Ronnie [Pearson – the drummer in Last Exit]
> up and say 'I've got an afternoon off next week if you wanna
> come in' – 'cause he let us record there for free.[9]

This was verified by Richardson and Wood, who regarded Last
Exit as a 'hot group', who in the early days were a 'splinter group
of Newcastle Big Band'.[10]

Discussing the quality of the Impulse Sound Recording Studio
recordings, Hedley stated,

> it's difficult for you, as everyone who is around who was a
> witness does not really want to talk about it. No one has got a
> very high opinion of what came out. Sting was totally embar-
> rassed for a long time, he would not even admit to being part
> of it.[11]

Indeed, when Hedley was approached around 2004 about the viability of releasing some of the recordings, he stated,

> I cannot think of a single track in that collection I would want to see the light of day . . . we were all coming from different points of view [musically], the music had not really got an identity by then.[12]

These points are verified by Sting in his autobiography – he believed there was 'nothing in those early Last Exit tapes to indicate anything but the floundering of an inexperienced group working without the help of a producer'.[13]

Keith Nichol took over the house engineer/producer role at Impulse from Mickey Sweeney in June 1980, remaining in the role for the next 22 years, until the studio's closure in 2002. Although not involved in the original Last Exit recordings, he was asked to safeguard them by transferring the data from the original quarter-inch tape, which had become brittle. Nichol recalled Sting visiting Impulse one last time in 1984 for a recording session, when Nichol was approached to engineer a track which was to become 'Moon over Bourbon Street', and eventually to be featured on Sting's first solo album – *The Dream of the Blue Turtles* (1984). After initiating a demo of the track in London consisting mainly of synthesizers, Sting arrived in Wallsend with the intention of 'merging some of the North East' into the track.[14] Nichol believed that 'he had this idea for a tune that was very trad jazz, very New Orleans jazz'.[15] The concept behind the track was to start off with local band the River City Jazzmen, who would portray not only a New Orleans jazz feel, but tie in with his Newcastle heritage. The idea was then gradually to 'morph from that kind of jazz into an "Englishman in New York" kind of jazz feel'.[16] Obviously using the recording studio space as a creative tool, Sting, not liking the original London demo, asked Nichol to erase it and have the River City Jazzmen re-record the entire song in a different key. Sting then took the recording away to work on it further, although when listening to the final released version, Nichol could not detect any of the recording activity that took place at Impulse. I have managed to get an exclusive listen to this Impulse demo that Nichol was referring to, and it is indeed heavily influenced by the New Orleans genre: it has the classic trombone, clarinet and trumpet combination performing contrapuntal lines throughout the performance, weaving in and around Sting's vocal line. Although the chord progression, lyrics and melody are identical to the final version, as Nichol states above, there is little evidence in the arrangement of the original Impulse recording on the version that made *The Dream of the Blue Turtles*, although it maintains a jazz feel, albeit with Baroque-style counterpoint as opposed to trad jazz. Aside from the humorous 'werewolf howling', which is on both versions, perhaps the most

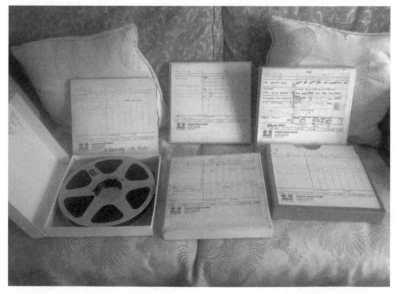

Selection of the original Last Exit demos recorded at Impulse Sound Recording Studio.

noticeable remnant is the improvised line intertwining with Sting's vocal, although the later version was performed by a solo soprano saxophone as opposed to trombone, clarinet and trumpet counterpoint.

Regarding Sting's recording activities prior to joining The Police, 29 individual Last Exit recorded songs have been identified, not including several which were recorded on more than one occasion and a number of unnamed instrumentals.[17] Although Gerry Richardson and Terry Ellis composed some (nine and three, respectively), the vast majority of the songs are penned by Sting – fifteen compositions in total. There are also two cover versions, which provide a useful insight into what was an important part of their live set. Gerry Richardson confirmed that guitarist John Hedley performed on all of the Impulse recordings in Wallsend, while Terry Ellis features on all of the London-based Pathway sessions. This was an important piece of information when attempting to ascertain when the Impulse and Pathway recordings took place, in addition to which songs were recorded where. Since Hedley left Last Exit in late October 1975, this confirmed that the Impulse recordings took place prior to this date.

Richardson was eager to point out that aside from the 'Whispering Voices' single, which was released in November 1975, neither the Impulse nor the Pathway recordings were intended for commercial release: the Impulse output was intended to be sold at gigs such as the San Sebastian Jazz Festival in 1975, while the Pathway sessions were used as demo recordings and paid for by Virgin, as part of Last Exit's newly acquired publishing deal. In his autobiography, Sting describes the publishing contract as very much 'Last Exit's', although as the principal songwriter and only member to go on to significant commercial success, the dubious details of a '50–50' deal only really had an impact on him. While the contract on the surface was a 'significant step toward realizing [Last Exit's] dream', it would result in a feud between Sting and

Virgin owner Richard Branson, which was not fully resolved until 1982.[18]

Since many of the Last Exit recordings have no precise date or recording venue details, some detective work was required in order to determine where and when they were recorded. So first, according to Sting's website, Last Exit produced a nine-track demo cassette recording entitled *First from Last Exit* in July 1975, just prior to their visit to the San Sebastian Jazz Festival on 16 July.[19] Recorded at Impulse, five of the songs were composed by Sting ('Truth Kills', 'Carrion Prince', 'Savage Beast', 'I Got It Made' and 'O My God'), the others having been composed by Gerry Richardson ('Whispering Voices', 'We Got Something', 'I'm on this Train' and 'A Bit of Peace'). The information on Sting's website also reveals a few indicative recording dates, such as 23 February 1975, when 'I Got It Made' was recorded, 7 March 1975, when 'I'm on this Train' was recorded, and 3 April 1975, when the now-famous 'O My God' was recorded.[20]

Before discussing the Pathway recordings, it is important to point out that Last Exit recorded a four-song demo at Impulse towards the end of 1974 – prior to the *First from Last Exit* demo.[21] It contained the following songs, two of which are composed by Sting: 'Every Day Is Just the Same' (Sting), 'Carrion Prince' (Sting), 'Don't Let It Bring You Down' (Neil Young cover) and 'Whispering Voices' (Gerry Richardson).[22] The original Impulse reel-to-reel recording for these songs occupies the same tape as folk band Five Hand Reel, a Scottish/Irish group who recorded their first album *Five Hand Reel* (1976) at the Studio for Impulse-based Rubber Records. As the tape is dated 7 January 1976, the Five Hand Reel sessions obviously took place after those of Last Exit – the fact they are occupying the same tape reflects the 'low importance' of Last Exit at that time.

Thanks to Impulse owner David Wood, who graciously supplied a CD of selected Last Exit master recordings, it has been possible to

Date: 7/1/76	Ref:				Tracks			
Titles	1	2	3	4	5	6	7	8
REEL REGGAE	BANJO / BANJO	FIDDLE / FIDDLE	BASSES / FIDDLE	GUITS VOICE	←DRUMS→ VOICES / XXX		6/TRACK <TRACK>	/TRACK
EVERYDAY'S JUST THE SAME TAKE 2	VOX	GIT	PIANO	BASS	DRUMS		VOX	VOX
CARRION PRINCE TAKE 2	GIT	GIT	PIANO	BASS	DRUMS		VOX	PERC
DON'T LET IT BRING YOU DOWN	VOX	VOX PIANO/SAX	PIANO	BASS	DRUMS		AZZ	CYMB
WHISPERING VOICES	GIT.	VOX GIT	PIANO	BASS	DRUMS		VOX	GIT

Artists: FIVE HAND REEL	Producer/Engineer:	Client: RUBBER
8 Track [X]	4 Track	15 ips [X]	Master [X]	Copy	EQ. NAB/CCIR	Dolby

Impulse Sound Studio
71 High Street East
Wallsend NE28 7RJ

Original reel-to-reel recording of first Last Exit recordings owned by David Wood.

listen to a selection of the original Last Exit material from the studio in high quality, most of the songs having been composed by Sting and released on the *First from Last Exit* cassette. These recordings solve any dispute in terms of where these songs are recorded. The tracks supplied by Wood comprised the following:

'Carrion Prince' (Sting): as on *First from Last Exit*
'Don't Let It Bring You Down' (Neil Young): as on the cassette demo of 1974
'I Got It Made' (Sting): as on *First from Last Exit*
'Every Day Is Just the Same' (Sting): as on the cassette demo of 1974

'O My God' (Sting): as on *First from Last Exit*

'I'm on this Train' (Gerry Richardson): as on *First from Last Exit*

'A Bit of Peace' (Gerry Richardson): as on *First from Last Exit*[23]

All of the Impulse tracks made available by David Wood are mixed with Sting's lead vocal in the centre of the mix, the electric piano/Hammond organ panned right and the rhythm guitar either central or to the left – a similar position to when they played live. Sting sings on the majority of the tracks, with some mixes such as 'Don't Let It Bring You Down' and 'O My God' clearly featuring a double-tracked lead vocal part.[24] John Hedley recalled double tracking and the use of reverb being on the vocals to hide intonation issues. Although one can hear this in the recordings, these recordings took place under pressured circumstances, with no opportunity to re-record specific parts the band were not happy with. Although Sting's vocals are easily identified, some of his bass parts are noticeably more virtuosic than his work with The Police, with the song 'I Got It Made', for example, appearing to have been influenced by Back Door's Colin Hodgkinson and Tower of Power's Rocco Prestia.

As a contextual backdrop for the Pathway recordings, according to the Phil Sutcliffe-penned article in *Sounds* magazine published in January 1977, it appears that Last Exit entered the studio for a three-day period to record thirteen tracks for Virgin. Sting subsequently described the space as 'not much better than the studio in Wallsend . . . a tiny room somewhat smaller than the circumference it takes to swing a cat, with an even tinier control room'.[25] Producer Tony Harris, who recorded at Pathway in 1992, confirmed this perspective:

> You get a pretty good idea of the size of the place from the outside shot, what you see is the total width of the place, it

was pretty much a two-storey garden shed. [The] total floor area of the studio and the control room can't have been much more than 12 foot by 12 foot [3.7 m × 3.7 m] . . . Upstairs [which was] reached by what would be more accurately described as a ladder than a staircase, was a small office, a tape store and the cupboard for the EMT plate reverb. As you came into the studio there was an upright piano on your right, then in the far right corner there was the control room, which was about 6 foot × 6 foot [2 m × 2 m] at most, with a tiny ledge where you could possibly park one buttock whilst you listened to playbacks.[26]

Pathway: located down an alleyway at the back of number 2 Grosvenor Avenue.

Although no date is mentioned in Phil Sutcliffe's *Sounds* article, he is referring to an 'extended' recording session that probably took place between 21 and 24 September 1976 (commencing the day after the band supported Isaac Guillory at Dingwalls in London), with the movement between north and south being the focus of the article. However, Sutcliffe does not mention an earlier one-day session at Pathway that occurred five months before. In his autobiography, Sting remembers this inaugural recording as taking place four days before his wedding, which was on 1 May 1976, making the date of the first visit to Pathway 27 April.

> Carol [Wilson – from Virgin] wants us to come to London and record some songs with a view to signing us to a publishing deal, hopefully as a first step to securing the band a recording deal.[27]

Although the precise details of this initial recording are very limited, Sting does recall laying down around ten tracks in the afternoon:

> We just play through the songs as if we are performing a live show, using none of the multi-tracking facilities to layer the sound.[28]

The bootleg CD, the inaccurately titled *Sting Last Exit Impulse Studio Demos*, appears to be comprised of the tracks recorded on this day, with the only exceptions being the first two songs – 'Carrion Prince' and 'Every Day Is Just the Same' – which were both recorded at Impulse. The Pathway tracks recorded on 27 April 1976 can therefore be estimated to be as follows, with all of the vocal pieces having been composed by Sting:[29]

'Night in the Grand Hotel' (Sting)
'Don't You Look at Me' (Sting)
'Fool in Love' (Sting)
'I Burn for You' (Sting)
'I'm on this Train' (alternative take) (Sting)
'Savage Beast' (alternative take) (Sting)
'Soul Music' (Sting)
'Untitled Instrumental 1' (Terry Ellis)
'Untitled Instrumental 2' (Terry Ellis)

The above nine tracks broadly comply with Sting's account of the number of songs recorded, although songs such as 'Night in the Grand Hotel', 'Savage Beast', 'Don't You Look at Me' and 'Fool in Love' clearly have some basic overdubs included.[30] When working out what other songs were recorded at Pathway, a useful piece of evidence was to emerge – a Last Exit Pathway recording, dated 8 October 1976. This comprised the following tracks:

'Truth Kills Everybody' (alternative take of 'Truth Kills')
    (Sting)
'Don't You Believe Me Baby' (Sting)
'Silence is Killing' (Gerry Richardson)
'A Bit of Peace' (alternative take) (Gerry Richardson)
'Chops and Chips' (Terry Ellis)
'O My God' (alternative take) (Sting)
'The Bed's too Big without You' (Sting)

This recording, marked as 'reel 2 of 2' on the cover and engineered by 'Barry and Pete', pieces together the majority of the Last Exit songs we are aware of, the only other titles 'missing' – aside from unnamed instrumentals – being the following: 'Don't Give Up on your Daytime Job' (Sting), 'I Can't Say' (Sting) and

'Give and Take' (Gerry Richardson). It can only be presumed these were part of the same session, but recorded on the first reel.

Although the combined list of Pathway recordings comprises nineteen songs on the surface, when one takes away the five alternative takes, one is left with fourteen songs – broadly in line with the number outlined in Phil Sutcliffe's *Sounds* article from 1977. What is interesting about this list is that Sting has unquestionably emerged as the dominant songwriter, composing eleven of the nineteen songs in total.

Of the recordings that are available from both Impulse and Pathway, there is virtually no evidence of reggae on any of the

The second of two Last Exit Pathway Master recordings, dated 8 October 1976.

recordings – either compositionally or in Sting's vocal qualities. However, Impulse owner David Wood did introduce Last Exit to reggae when asking the band to cover 'Put on your Wings and Fly' – he suggested they 'take a shot at it skank style'.[31] Although there was little evidence of the style when listening to the recording, this is an interesting early venture into the music that would define The Police. Discussing the song, Phil Sutcliffe and Hugh Fielder commented,

> The strange thing was that, according to Gerry [Richardson], Dave [Wood] wouldn't let Sting sing it at first and eventually recorded it with him in duet with Ronnie. Gerry's verdict: 'It was awful'. It was never released and Sting's budding sympathy with natty rhythms was further rebuffed when Ronnie [Pearson] refused to play a reggae song he wrote for Last Exit, 'Let Me Do It to You'.[32]

Despite these early engagements, this helps confirm that reggae was an influence that Sting assimilated fairly rapidly during the early years of living in London.

During what can be heard of both the Impulse and Pathway recordings, it is obvious that Last Exit had a sound palette which was limited by cost, although one can hear clear influences of 'expensively produced' American jazz-rock artists, in particular The Crusaders, Tower of Power and Return to Forever. 'Every Day Is Just the Same' and 'Don't You Look at Me' have a clear Latin American influence, which Sting would later explore in songs such as 'Send your Love', 'Shape of my Heart', 'La Belle Dame sans Regrets' and 'All Would Envy', in addition to his EP *Nada Como el Sol* of 1988.[33] There are also a couple of untitled instrumental songs (described by the author as 'Instrumental 1' and 'Instrumental 2') composed by Terry Ellis, which are more directly influenced by the jazz-rock movement. The timing

of these compositions was unfortunate due to the impending
emergence of punk, which was to replace jazz-rock forcibly in
the public's (and record companies') consciousness over the next
twelve months. As with the Impulse-recorded 'I Got It Made',
Pathway's 'Soul Music' is noticeably influenced by Back Door's
Colin Hodgkinson, featuring the rhythmic percussive style of the
older player. 'Put on Your Wings and Fly' and 'Don't Let It Bring
you Down' are the only cover versions in the available combined
collections, the latter being a 'jazz funk' version of a Neil Young
song, dominated texturally by a Fender Rhodes, an instrument
heavily associated with jazz fusion of the early 1970s. In addition
to providing a snapshot of one of the countless Last Exit cover
versions they performed live, this song features Sting's capacity to
add momentum to a song by progressing from his 'chest voice',
to his now-famous falsetto high vocal as the song progresses.[34] His
capacity to do this during the Last Exit years is also evidenced on
songs such as 'I Burn for You' and 'Night in the Grand Hotel'.[35]

In his autobiography, Sting discusses writing most of the
songs for The Police's first album between August and Christmas
1977, recollecting,

> salvaging fragments of songs written for [Last Exit] and morph-
> ing them into new chords and melodies. The new songs are
> more direct, more economic than their old incarnations, but
> balanced with a subtlety the band hadn't explored before.[36]

Based on our knowledge of the songs Sting composed for Last
Exit, he appears to be talking about the songs listed below, which
can be subdivided into three sections: those that were reworked
and released on albums or singles by The Police or during Sting's
solo career; those that were reworked and recorded as demos
for potential release; and those that were performed in early live
performances of The Police.

Songs reworked and released on albums or singles

'Savage Beast'
'I Burn for You'
'Carrion Prince'
'O My God'
'Fool in Love'
'Truth Kills' / 'Truth Kills Everybody'
'The Bed's too Big without You'

Songs recorded to demo-quality and considered for release

'Don't Give Up on your Daytime Job'[37]
'Don't You Believe me Baby'[38]
'Don't You Look at Me'[39]

Songs performed in early performances by The Police

'Night at the Grand Hotel'

Of the seven songs that were commercially released, three ('I Burn for You', 'O My God' and 'The Bed's too Big without You') kept their original titles, focusing on two themes that were to become pervasive in Sting's creative output – lonely, often tortured, romantic relationships and religion. 'Fool in Love', which also has a 'tortured love relationship' theme, undertook more comprehensive changes to its melody and harmony, in addition to changing its title to the now-famous 'So Lonely'. 'Savage Beast' was also renamed, becoming 'We Work the Black Seam', and although this song retained much of its original melody, the new lyrical content aligns more closely with Sting's socialist tendencies.[40] 'Carrion Prince' was extended and elaborated upon to become 'Bring on the Night', as recorded on *Reggatta de Blanc*

(1979), and *Bring on the Night* (1986). Of all the songs that were commercially released, 'Truth Kills' / 'Truth Kills Everybody' arguably undergoes the most comprehensive changes, the style changing from a mid-tempo ballad to an up-tempo punk rock piece. Since the harmony and melody are also totally differ-ent, the only real similarity is the title (which became 'Truth Hits Everybody', as recorded on *Outlandos d'Amour*) and very small sections of the lyrics, Sting clearly using the 'open doors' metaphor from the original, in addition to highlighting the word 'truth' – only this time it 'hits' everybody rather than 'kills', a decision that may have been made for commercial reasons.[41] By far the most significant phrase lifted from the original is the lyrics of the bridge.

Regarding the Last Exit songs that never made commercial release but were considered, all were contemplated for *Ghost in the Machine* and all have titles beginning with the letter D. Of the two Last Exit songs it has been possible to hear ('Don't You Look at Me' and 'Don't Give Up on your Daytime Job'), it is apparent, when listening to the demos, that both bear strong similarities to the original Last Exit recordings from a lyrical, melodic and harmonic perspective.[42] Although information regarding early performances of The Police is sparse, examination of available bootlegs reveals that 'Night at the Grand Hotel' was included in the set. In spite of the fact that the style of this song in itself is basically an 'old-fashioned' blues, it would have been an easy number to learn – and probably considered a set filler.[43]

Of the fifteen songs that Sting composed for Last Exit, only four were not re-recorded in some format and/or performed live in his subsequent career: 'Every Day Is Just the Same', 'I Can't Say', 'I Got It Made' and 'Soul Music'. Though this is pure specu-lation, it appears that these songs either had no lyrical content that reflected the new direction of The Police, or the funk/Latin-based rhythms simply sounded out of date.[44]

Some of Sting's Last Exit recordings are excellent indicators of how his songs with The Police and solo career became more direct, economic and balanced. These Last Exit songs were chosen for discussion because they all progressed from being performed and recorded at a local level to having significant commercial success, consequently providing a useful insight into Sting's creative processes.

'I BURN FOR YOU'

'I Burn for You' is the only track of the five selected that has remained largely unaltered in its later versions, which have been featured on albums such as *Bring on the Night* (1986), *Symphonicities* (2010) and *Sting 25 Years* (2011), in addition to an earlier version recorded by The Police, as performed in Sting's movie *Brimstone and Treacle* (1982). The song has also been recorded by artists such as Anna Maria Jopek, Kevyn Lettau and Julienne Taylor, all of whom undertake alternative arrangements of the song – as opposed to attempting to copy the original versions directly.[45]

The original Last Exit demo features keyboards, bass and drums and is the only song listened to that does not feature guitar. Sting's somewhat cryptic statement in his autobiography that 'it wouldn't take a genius to identify the source of [the song's] inspiration' strongly alludes to the likelihood that the song was written in Newcastle and was essentially an ode to Frances Tomelty – as with 'The Bed's too Big without You'.[46] This theme of the tortured consequences of romantic relationships was one Sting would return to in *Outlandos d'Amour*, in songs such as 'Can't Stand Losing You' and 'So Lonely', and in his later solo career in songs such as 'Fortress around my Heart' from *The Dream of the Blue Turtles*. At nearly twice the duration of the Last Exit original, the *Bring on the Night* version progresses into an extended improvised section via a key change in the final verse, with Sting ad-libbing around the refrain ('I Burn for You') which eventually progresses into a vocal, bass and soprano saxophone solo. The *Bring on the Night* version was recorded live in Arnhem as part of his initial solo career world tour, commencing and ending with a Steve Reich-influenced repeated loop on guitar and keyboards. Aside from the key change in the final verse, the introduction of the above-mentioned melody and the ad-lib ending, the general texture of these versions is heavily influenced by the Last Exit original. Although there is no concrete proof, it would appear that the earlier version by The Police was built around the instrumentation and membership of the band, whose guitar-centric sound was not the ideal sonic texture to represent the protagonist of the song. The emphasis of the repeated block guitar chords on this version reduces the textural sparseness featured on the other versions, which somehow heightens the impact of the tormented loneliness of the protagonist. Although all of the later versions are far longer than the original, they omit a bridge section, which occurred between the second and third verses. Sting obviously decided, when re-recording the song with The Police, that the lyric and accompanying melodic change were not required – possibly to avoid breaking up the repetition between sections that help depict the obsessional undercurrent of the song, a factor which is accentuated in the *Bring on the Night* version via the interlocking loops on guitar and keyboards.

'CARRION PRINCE'

Based on the title of the Ted Hughes poem 'King of Carrion', the two versions of 'Carrion Prince' were recorded at Impulse.[47] The song was eventually to become known as 'Bring on the Night' – as documented on both The Police's second album, *Reggatta de Blanc* (1979), and then, as with 'I Burn for You', Sting's live album *Bring on the Night*. Although there are not as many cover versions of this song as there are of 'I Burn for You', the track was featured in an instrumental 'dub' mix on *The Police in Dub*, an album which incorporates a number of other songs by The Police into this genre.[48] The track list on the front of the original Impulse recordings reveals that the 'Take 2' recording features two guitars (occupying a track each), drums (occupying two tracks), piano and percussion (occupying a track each), with Sting's bass recorded on track four and his vocal on track seven. As with all of the Newcastle-based songs that were eventually to be appropriated by Sting at a later date, the original track was engineered by Mickey Sweeny, produced by Dave Wood and featured John Hedley on guitar, Gerry Richardson on keyboards and Ronnie Pearson on drums. The original versions of both takes of the song seem influenced by the more commercial side of the jazz-rock movement the band was aspiring to at the time.

Regarding 'Take 2', after an introduction consisting of a repeated melody on guitar and piano with an underlying bass line, the song progresses to be noticeably similar melodically to 'Bring on the Night' – although with key differences. First, the version by The Police has been appropriated to the 'white reggae' style, Sting's syncopated bass being a notable reason behind this stylistic shift, particularly in the chorus, in which it is accompanied with the 'skank' guitar style of Andy Summers. Comparing both versions, it becomes apparent that the second half of the verses of the Last Exit original are not used in the later version by The Police – possibly because it was considered to be too harmonically complex to comply with the reggae style and the commercial impact they were hoping to achieve. On this point, the original versions have no chorus, comprising only a repeated sequence of verses. Although the addition of a chorus on The Police version undoubtedly imbues the song with more commerciality, biographer Christopher Gable asserted that 'Sting and [Andy] Summers weren't quite sure what to make of the chorus' in The Police version, proceeding to state that Sting was reported to have said that he had always hated it.[49] Although it is difficult to read into this comment, might it be that Sting was comparing it to a more favourable Last Exit original, which was written prior to considerations of commercial impact? Gable does provide a useful account of how Sting musically addresses the 'issues' with the chorus when recording the later 'Bring on the Night', making the necessary changes so it is 'harmonically clarified'.[50] Both Last Exit's and The Police's versions have guitar solos, although the latter is understandably more 'produced' than the former – again having more commercial intent.

Lyrically, both verses of The Police's adaptation are clearly influenced by the original, the first verse of each commencing with identical lyrics, melody and harmony. The lyrics in the second verse of The Police's version are not identical, but very similar. Comparing the two sets of lyrics, it is apparent that the Last Exit arrangements are more ambiguous, having an almost-metaphysical feel to them, but with the replacement of the word 'universe' with 'future', The Police's rendition relates more directly to the song's protagonist, wishing for the passing of daytime so s/he can hide. It is noticeable also how the chord sequence at the end of the *Bring on the Night* version is more akin to Last Exit's, a factor that fits in with Christopher Sandford's belief that Sting's solo career is representative of what Last Exit could have sounded like.[51]

'SAVAGE BEAST'

The two versions of 'Savage Beast' were probably recorded around a year apart at Impulse and Pathway, respectively. Under the song's new name, 'We Work the Black Seam', it first appeared on *The Dream of the Blue Turtles* in 1985, before appearing on *Bring on the Night* and *Symphonicities*. Although its likenesses may not be as immediately obvious as those of the previous two songs,

'Savage Beast' does have a strong lyrical similarity to its later
incarnations, which increases as the song progresses. It also incorporates the exact melody and a very similar chord progression
for the verses. Like 'Carrion Prince', 'Savage Beast' has no chorus
section, opting to evolve into an extended vamp-based guitar
solo. As mentioned above, the lack of a chorus has the potential
to reduce the commercial appeal of a pop song – so this possibly
explains the subsequent inclusion of a chorus and refrain in 'We
Work the Black Seam'. Both versions of 'Savage Beast' are broadly
similar in terms of construction, the Pathway recording being
around 52 seconds longer, due to an extended guitar solo (which
is over a single chord as opposed to a two chord vamp) and a
longer introduction. The Pathway recording also has the guitar
more centrally featured, in terms of melodic content, and uses a
guitar finger-picking section during two of the verses, which has
a similar sound to later Sting compositions such as 'Bring on the
Night' and 'Shape of my Heart'. The Impulse version of the song
features Sting's voice almost double tracked using a slap-back
echo effect with a small delay panned to the left in the stereo
spectrum. While Sting's bass is positioned centrally, the guitar and
electric piano parts are panned right and left, giving the recording
a greater sense of space. As opposed to occupying a static space
in the stereo mix, the guitar solo of this mix commences on the
right, before moving to the left and back again.

'Savage Beast' is a song of loneliness, and 'We Work the
Black Seam' is related very closely to Sting's socialist tendencies
through the lens of the miners' strike of 1984; the songs' subjects
therefore appear very different on the surface. Although both
songs are sung in the first person, Sting firmly positions himself
as 'one of the community of miners' in 'We Work the Black
Seam', as opposed to being an isolated and 'lonely savage beast'.
The changes brought about by the miners' strike of 1984–5 had
a profound impact in Newcastle, including on Sting's hometown

of Wallsend, so it is supposed that the strong melodic theme of 'Savage Beast' was something that Sting was keen to align with more meaningful lyrics. Once Sting's career became established, the miners' strike provided the ideal cultural backdrop to inspire this change, taking place during the same period as he was recording *The Dream of the Blue Turtles*.

Upon closer examination of the lyric, Sting reuses some of the phrases from 'Savage Beast' somehow to comply with the very different context of 'We Work the Black Seam'. It is apparent that the two verses of 'Savage Beast' are nearly identical to verses five and six of the *Symphonicities* and *Bring on the Night* versions of 'We Work the Black Seam'. For example, 'I cling onto this mountain while I sleep' becomes '*You* cling onto your mountain while we sleep', both of which bear a loose similarity to William Blake's poem 'And Did Those Feet in Ancient Time', which opens with the line 'And did those feet in ancient time / Walk upon England's mountains green.' The poem is, of course, referring to the apocryphal mythological story of a young Jesus visiting Glastonbury and the building of a New Jerusalem 'in England's green and pleasant land'. Although it is conjecture to consider what Sting actually meant by these references, the word 'mountain' may initially have alluded to the protagonist – the 'Savage Beast' – clinging on to some sort of hope, while in 'We Work the Black Seam', it could allude to the Conservative government's future perception of a 'New Jerusalem' – which did not include the long-standing coal industry of Newcastle. What is clear is that both verses of the original song have been carefully altered to adhere to the new subject.[52]

'O MY GOD'

The Impulse version of 'O My God' was recorded on 3 April 1975. Labelled 'O My Gawd' on the master tape, the instrumentation occupies six of the available eight studio tracks, with Sting's bass once again on track four and two vocal parts recorded on tracks seven to eight. As with a number of other tracks recorded by Last Exit at Impulse, Sting's vocals are double tracked – with both voices singing nearly identical melody lines. Although this is a common production technique in order to acquire a full vocal sound, it appears that in the Last Exit recordings, either this device is used to cover up performance issues or the mix is a combination of an actual take and a 'guide vocal', which was accidentally included in the final mix. Whatever the reason, it results in a slightly distant, almost unearthly sound in the vocal line. After Sting's solo bass guitar introduction, the texture of the Impulse recording is dominated by a Hammond organ, resulting in a gospel feel, which adds an ironic twist to the lyrical subject matter of a God who is accused of being distant. Like 'I Burn for You', the subject of this song has not changed in the version recorded by The Police on *Synchronicity* in 1983 – it being essentially a gripe against God. A large portion of the lyrics of The Police's version has been taken from the Last Exit original, with a couple of new insertions – verses six and eight, which are a direct lyrical quote from 'Every Little Thing She Does Is Magic' (*Ghost in the Machine*, 1981). This purposeful self-referencing of his own work can also be found in songs such as 'Dead Man's Rope' and 'We'll Be Together', but in this case, the song references both Sting's time in Newcastle and his other work with The Police simultaneously. [53]

Synchronicity was to become The Police's most commercially successful album, being put forward for five Grammy awards and winning three. Stylistically, the gospel feel has been removed, with the chord sequence once again being simplified. This definitive version of 'O My God' has also had a bridge section added, which has a bass line reminiscent of 'Twist and Shout' by the Beatles; at one point towards the end of the song, this is combined with the above-mentioned reference to 'Every Little Thing She Does Is

Magic'.[54] Although no cover versions of 'O My God' were found, bands such as Guns N' Roses, The Kaiser Chiefs and Jay-Z, among numerous others, have used the title for their own songs.[55] The song was recorded again by Last Exit in 1976 at Pathway, but it has not been possible to listen to this recording.

'FOOL IN LOVE'

Though it is difficult to detect the similarity if one does not listen carefully, it quickly becomes apparent that 'Fool in Love' uses the same lyrical content in the verses as 'So Lonely' does, but with an entirely different melody and chord progression. As opposed to previous practices outlined above, in which the post-Last Exit versions tended to add a chorus to a repeated verse, 'So Lonely' simply incorporates a new chorus in 'Fool in Love', which just emphasizes repeatedly that the protagonist of the song is 'So Lonely'. Stylistically, the Last Exit song is mid-tempo funk throughout, complete with soon-to-be-dated wah-wah guitar in the verses, while the song by The Police shifts between reggae for the verses and rock in the choruses. This reggae/rock combination is a technique Sting would employ on other early Police songs such as 'Roxanne' and 'Can't Stand Losing You'. Sting developed a tendency during his years with The Police to juxtapose seemingly 'sad' lyrical content with more up-tempo, 'happier' background music – adding what can be described as a 'split personality' element to his music that arguably aligned with the way his personal characteristics were developing at the time. Although stylistically very different, both 'Fool in Love' and 'So Lonely' do this, the lyrical content being far more sombre than the musical styles. Sting provides his own harmony parts in both instances, the Last Exit song demonstrating an early example of this practice. 'So Lonely' has subsequently had a number of rearrangements, such as those by Novaspace (*Barcatronics*, 2005) and Eve St Jones

(*Coffee and Memories*, 2014), but arguably the most interesting is the version by Nouvelle Vague (*3*, 2009), who slows the tempo down and makes the harmonic backing more static in places. In doing so, she aligns the lyrical content with the musical, thus avoiding the 'split personality' inherent in Sting's versions.

These recordings in many ways represent Sting's final gestures as a musician based in the northeast of England, as he was soon to fulfil his ambition and make the long journey south, to a new stage of his career based in London.

PART 2: **LONDON AND BEYOND**

5 THE POLICE

Having made the decision to move south, Sting was not only
following in the tradition of fellow Geordie musicians such as
Hank Marvin, Eric Burdon and Bryan Ferry, but authors such as
Jack Common, who had made the journey against the wishes
of his father in 1928 in order to improve his chances of gaining
meaningful employment. However, the imperative to find work is
a universal phenomena, with the immigration of peoples taking
place not only within countries, but across nations. Indeed, Sting's
journey south has to be regarded as the first stage of future movements, which eventually culminated in his current status as a world
citizen, owning and living in multiple homes around the world.

After performing one of Last Exit's final gigs in the northeast
of England at Newcastle University Theatre on 3 December 1976,
Sting set off for London in January 1977 with his wife Frances
Tomelty, his baby son Joe and 'a couple of bags of clothes, two
guitars and a wicker rocking chair' – his worldly belongings.[1]
Their financial future was at that point unknown, but this
decision to leave his security as a provincial schoolteacher and
part-time musician was pivotal, not only in terms of his forth-
coming projection into megastardom, but for guaranteeing that
songs such as 'The Bed's too Big without You', 'I Burn for You'
and 'O My God' were not condemned to northern folklore,
and were instead to become a well-known part of popular
culture throughout the world. Indeed, according to Sting's

autobiography, the final song Last Exit performed in Newcastle was entitled 'Don't Give Up on your Daytime Job', an irony that would have resonated with the band profoundly at this crucial point in their respective careers.

Although the band members of Last Exit intended to follow him to London, the security of well-paid, albeit not particularly glamorous, regular work, in addition to family commitments of some members, was eventually to result in the band splitting up – opening up the way for Sting to begin the London stage of his career.[2] Last Exit did perform in London on many occasions during late 1976 and into early 1977. For example, there is a free-admission lunchtime concert noted at the London School of Economics in Aldwych on 12 November 1976 and a performance at the Nashville Room on 22 December 1976, while on 21 January 1977, they supported Kites, also at the Nashville Room. Last Exit further supported Kevin Coyne on 22 January 1977 at the London School of Economics, the ticket stub stating the timing of the gig to be '7.30 Till Late'.[3] The gigs in January are particularly inter-esting, as they take place at a time during which Sting had just moved to London, had already formed a relationship with Stewart Copeland and was effectively working with both Last Exit and early incarnations of The Police. Indeed, newspaper coverage in *The Melody Maker* reveals that Last Exit was performing in London as late as Sunday 27 February 1977, when they performed at the Red Cow in Hammersmith – only two days prior to the inaugural performance of The Police.

So having served his apprenticeship in the pubs and clubs of the northeast of England, Sting arrived in London, signed up for unemployment benefit at Lisson Grove NW1 and started another season of paying his musical dues – a process which included sleeping on friends' floors and in rented apartments, and doing low-paid gigs at what he describes as 'flea-pit hotels'.[4] All of these factors would eventually influence his creative output.[5]

Newspaper cutting of Last Exit performing at the Red Cow on Sunday 27 February 1977.

After initially being introduced to Stewart Copeland by the journalist Phil Sutcliffe in Newcastle the day after a Curved Air gig at Newcastle Polytechnic on 24 September 1976, Sting made a point of re-engaging with Copeland soon after moving to London, at his then residence, the top floor of 26 Green Street, Mayfair, which had been appropriated as a squat with other members of Curved Air – including Copeland's eventual wife Sonja Kristina.[6] Sting described him as 'the most exciting drummer I've ever worked with', and his informal jam sessions with Copeland represent the beginning of a musical partnership – one that would ultimately change both of their lives.[7]

When Sting arrived in London, the music scene in the capital was in the middle of a transition that was disregarding the jazz-rock and progressive leanings of his previous band Last Exit and moving towards the DIY simplicity of bands such as The Sex Pistols, The Clash, Chelsea and The Damned. The aesthetic call of these groups was founded on a 'return to simplicity', rejecting the overproduced sound of bands such as Yes and Emerson, Lake & Palmer for the 'raw garage-band sound of the mid 1960s'.[8]

> John Covach: Punk rock, in an effort perhaps to establish a directness of personal expression, tended to celebrate musical amateurism, and clearly such an aesthetic is antithetical to the drive to virtuosity and textual complexity found in the music of most progressive groups.[9]

Covach is quick to point out, however, that much new wave music was often more complex than it appeared on the surface, citing Devo, Elvis Costello, Talking Heads and Joe Jackson as examples of more sophisticated artists. As we will see, the music of The Police also complies with this category, all three members being a considerable distance from the 'we want to be amateurs' rhetoric of Johnny Rotten.[10] The simplicity of the punk style is related to

Green Street, Mayfair: the roof terrace location where the photograph for the front cover of 'Fall Out' was taken.

Alternative take from the cover of 'Fall Out' on the roof terrace of 26 Green Street.

its basic formal design, its short duration, a lack of virtuosic solo-ing and somewhat predictable chord patterns, although it could be considered 'much more sophisticated in production terms than some progressive music of the same period'.[11] Although this comment is open to debate, what is clear is that these musical transformations were accompanied by social and cultural change. Britain was going through a series of depressing headlines that dominated the national press around the time Sting was moving to London: in 2004 the New Economics Foundation pronounced that 1976 was the 'best' British year in recent memory.[12] Basing their data on factors such as unemployment levels, narrowing of the wage gap, low interest rates and average household income, the findings provoked much debate in the national press. Although it highlighted positives, it also noted negatives:

> 1976 was also a year of strikes and raging inflation. The full scale of the economic failure the country was facing became evident, as Britain was forced into the humiliating position of asking international bankers to bail it out to the tune of bil-lions of pounds. Strikes in public services were just something people had to deal with. The standard rate of tax stood at 35 pence in the pound. Inflation raged at around 17%.[13]

In 2013 the *Daily Mirror* published an article that highlighted a shift in musical taste, which is seen to coincide with the 'hot summer of 1976':

> In the charts Brotherhood of Man's Eurovision winner Save All Your Kisses For Me and The Wurzels' Combine Harvester were firm favourites. Classic albums Hotel California by the Eagles and Stevie Wonder's Songs in the Key of Life were released in '76 but there were signs of a shift in musical tastes. A shocked nation saw the Sex Pistols' foul-mouthed

TV interview with Bill Grundy and The Damned released New Rose, widely regarded as the first punk single. Some saw punk as the death of pop but to others it was bringing music back to life while raising two fingers to the establishment.[14]

During the period that Sting moved out of Newcastle, punk was beginning to emerge as a recognizable style in London, the aforementioned bands carrying a mix of eclectic influences that reflected the social and cultural conditions of the time:

> Strands from David Bowie and glitter rock were woven together with elements from American proto punk (the Ramones, the Heartbreakers, Iggy Pop, Richard Hell), from that faction within London pub-rock (the 101-ers, the Gorillas, etc.).[15]

A major narrative of the British punk movement was that of alienation, a factor which is implicit not only in the lyrics and accompanying musical textures of songs such as The Sex Pistols' 'Pretty Vacant', but visually, with the postmodern cut-and-paste fashion accompanied by the expressionless faces of musicians in bands such as The Sex Pistols, The Vibrators and Sham 69. Although the musical and dress code origins of punk are complex, it is the movement's relationship with reggae that is of most interest when considering Sting. Although The Police were arguably not influenced by the style philosophically, they were musically, Sting's bass lines playing a prominent role in this relationship.[16] Discussing the 'connection between the energetic music of punk and more sophisticated musical forms', Sting commented,

> I wanted to take it [punk] and bridge a gap between the interesting chords and harmonic variations and this wild energy. And what eventually allowed me to do it was listening to

reggae. Bob Marley especially. I saw a rhythmic connection between the fast bass of punk and the holes of reggae. I got interested in trying to write songs that combined these apparently diverse styles.[17]

This mixture of space and 'busyness' was noticeably apparent in songs such as 'So Lonely', 'Roxanne' and 'Can't Stand Losing You' from *Outlandos d'Amour*, all of which simply juxtapose reggae-influenced verses with rock/punk choruses. Although these sudden changes could be considered crude, they do offer all three players the opportunity to display their advanced musicianship subtly. In Sting's case, they also enabled him to show a clear reggae influence in his vocal style, which up until this point had not been noticeable. Sting had not displayed any significant interest in reggae during his time in Newcastle, so this development has to be considered a 'London phenomenon'.[18] This was confirmed in discussion with ex-Gong bass player Mike Howlett:

In around late 1977 . . . I was around Sting's basement flat in Princess Square [Bayswater] and Stewart [Copeland] comes around – walking in carrying a pile of Bob Marley records. I remember him saying 'I'm going to turn you on to this guy' to Sting. And a year later they come out with *Reggatta de Blanc* . . . I have always said that was Stewart's vision . . . and Sting was this – kind of this raw talent who could sing, a competent musician and bass player [and a] very talented writer. But he needed to be pointed in a direction.[19]

Describing it as 'directed creativity', Howlett then proceeded to discuss how some musicians respond positively to being given a brief, which acts as the inspiration underpinning new songwriting material. It was arguably the introduction to reggae, so prominent on the early recordings of The Police, which acted as the creative and stylistic spark that provided Sting with a commercial context for his songwriting. As opposed to regarding this process as plagiarism, Sting was, in fact, continuing a long tradition of UK-based bands such as The Rolling Stones, The Animals and The Beatles, who absorbed the influences of Afro-American artists, before reappropriating the music into a contemporary style for new audiences.

So after having to sign on initially to receive unemployment benefit, it was to be only two months before Sting and The Police were not only formed, but were performing their first gig on 1 March 1977 – at the Alexandria Club, in Newport, Wales, with their first guitarist Henry Padovani. This was to be the start of several successive tours, in which they supported artists such as Cherry Vanilla, Johnny Thunders and the Heartbreakers, and Wayne County and the Electric Chairs. According to the Welsh concert promoter Jonny Perkins, who promoted this first gig at the Alexandria Club, around thirty audience members were present, The Police acting as support and backing band for the American artist Cherry Vanilla.[20]

> Cherry couldn't afford to bring her own band over, at the time, as this was her first ever British tour. So she used some British musicians who were looking for gigs . . . The Police had their first single out at the time, called Fallout. I paid Cherry £100 for the event, and she paid The Police £15.[21]

Looking at the publicity for the show in Perkins's book, it is noticeable that the name of 'The Police' is not mentioned, simply being noted as 'her band'. In the same article, Perkins pointed out that the name was considered controversial at the time:

> The Argus [a local newspaper] wouldn't advertise them as The Police, saying that the chief constable would be onto them

if they were to advertise The Police. The Argus would only advertise them as 'Her Band'.[22]

Sting, who names the club as 'Alexander's' in his autobiography, describes it as a 'shabby little nightclub . . . near a railway line'.[23] He continues:

> Inside the club is cold, damp, and dingy and there is a pungent smell of stale smoke and the sickly hop-infused stink of last week's beer . . . We set up the gear and PA on a tiny stage covered in angry cigarette burns and sticky underfoot with spilled drinks and old sweat. We will play scores of these clubs up and down the country, with dressing rooms no bigger than toilets.[24]

Speaking to Perkins, he described the club as being 'the last real nightclub in Newport', having a 'capacity of around 200' with a 'stage in the middle of the room'.[25] Moreover,

> there would be bouncers on the door and ladies of the night frequenting it . . . this is the reason I picked the place as it went well with the genre of music [punk] . . . But then I had to stop calling it punk, because once I had lost that venue [the Alexandria Club], if you mentioned punk to any of the other venues they would run a mile.[26]

The reactions by regional venues such as the Alexandria Club not wanting to stage punk music was a reflection of the way the music was portrayed in the national press at the time. Although by this point The Sex Pistols were yet to release *Never Mind the Bollocks, Here's the Sex Pistols*, which came out seven months later in October 1977, they had already released the single 'Anarchy in the UK' in November 1976, and had also created an uproar by

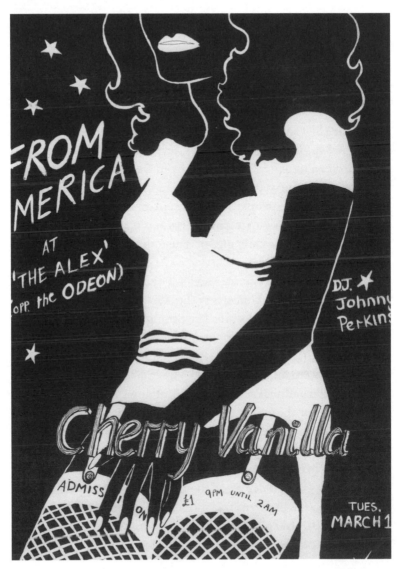

Poster of the first official gig by The Police at the Alexandria Club in Newport, Wales.

using foul language on Thames Television's *Today* programme the following month. This resulted in much negative publicity from national newspapers such as the *Daily Mirror* and the *Daily Telegraph*, who reported headlines of 'Fury at Filthy TV Chat' and '4 Letter Words Rock TV'.[27] Prior to this, in February 1977, a month before The Police performed in Newport, Wales, The Sex Pistols, alongside The Clash and Johnny Thunders and the Heartbreakers, performed at the Castle Cinema in Caerphilly, in what was described in a local fanzine as 'Anarchy in Caerphilly'. While the music was being played, the magazine reported there to be more than three hundred people, in addition to an accompanying police force outside the venue, singing 'Christmas Carols in protest to the concert'.[28] The early gigs of The Police were positioned within this social context.

In addition to the Cherry Vanilla/Police gig, Perkins only promoted three other concerts at the Alexandria Club in 1977 prior to its permanent closure: The Stranglers on 15 February, The Vibrators on 22 February and, finally, Wayne County and the Electric Chairs on 8 March. All of these bands were part of the punk movement that Sting and The Police used as a vehicle to obtain international success, and local newspaper adverts promoted all of these concerts as 'new wave rock' – presumably in an attempt to circumnavigate the negative press of the 'punk' label.[29] Sting's first performance in Newport comprised four sets, with The Police performing alternative sets with Cherry Vanilla.[30] Interestingly, Perkins described the music The Police performed that evening as being 'very jazz influenced' and having little resemblance to the sound they became famous for.[31] Although he does not specifically mention the music performed that night, Sting recalls,

> The Police set begins at ten to eleven and is finished on the stroke of the hour. It blisters along at such a pace – no gaps

between the songs, defying the audience to be critical or
appreciative . . . and then we're off before they know what's
hit them.[32]

A few weeks prior to performing their first gig in Newport, The
Police had recorded their first single, the punk-inspired 'Fall Out',
written by Stewart Copeland, produced by Copeland and Barry
Hammond (aka 'Bazza') and released in May 1977 on the 'Illegal
Records' label belonging to Stewart's brother, Miles Copeland.
The recording took place at Pathway Studios, 2a Grosvenor
Avenue, Islington, London N5, on 12 February and along with its
B-side, 'Nothing Achieving', these represent the only recordings to
feature the original guitarist Henry Padovani as part of the three
piece.[33] The eight-track Pathway Studios was, of course, the very
space in which Last Exit had recorded a selection of their demo
recordings for Virgin Records only a few months before.

Although the recording environment of Pathway was considered to be basic, the studio is now well known for the early
recordings of not only The Police, but of artists such as Squeeze
and Dire Straits.[34] The studio was founded by Mike Finesilver
and Peter Ker; the former co-wrote the classic song 'Fire' by The
Crazy World of Arthur Brown and used the royalties to purchase
the studio.[35] Originally opened in 1970, it was extensively used in
the mid-1970s by Stiff Records both to demo and to release products by artists such as Elvis Costello, The Damned, Lene Lovich
and Madness.[36]

According to Sting, the original front cover of 'Fall Out'
was pictured 'on the roof of the Copeland squat in Mayfair on a
bitterly cold and grey February afternoon'.[37] The black-and-white
image gives the record an authentic DIY look and actually adds to
the bleakness mentioned by Sting, a device used by other punk
artists of the time, such as The Ramones (*Ramones*, 1976) and The
Clash (*The Clash*, 1977).[38] Although Copeland's squat was actually

positioned in an affluent part of central London, just around the corner from Oxford Street, the rooftop view, combined with the black-and-white image, provides an edgy urban dimension to the photo. In the days prior to obtaining any financial remuneration for their music, the clothes the band members are wearing are not coordinated, Sting wearing a T-shirt and what appears to be a second-hand jacket top and Copeland a Ramones-type leather jacket.[39] The facial expressions of all three members could be described as solemn. At this point, the band had also not yet adopted their blond-haired image. The photographer of the 'Fall Out' session, Lawrence Impey, confirmed that the pictures were actually taken in January 1977, only a few weeks after Sting moved to London. Having gone to Millfield boarding school in Somerset with Stewart Copeland, Impey had already developed a long-term friendship with him by the time The Police formed in January 1977. Asked if he would be interested in doing the photo shoot for what would become 'Fall Out' on the rooftop of Copeland's squat in Green Street, Impey stated 'trust Stewart for having a squat in the middle of Mayfair . . . I love that, it's very, very Stewart . . . it says a lot about The Police, basically.'[40]

Remembering Sting that day, he continued,

> You can see he has got quite a different persona from the later Sting, the kind of tortured genius. He has always got his hand up to his forehead like the weight of the world is upon him, where there is one [picture] that I took up on the rooftop, where he has a great big grin – like a Cheshire cat . . . You could not get further away from his image today.[41]

The picture Impey is referring to depicts an ungroomed Sting, who has his bass guitar strapped around his neck with a thick guitar strap, and he wears what Impey recalls as being a borrowed jacket.

A smiling Sting on the rooftop of Green Street, during the 'Fall Out' photo shoot.

On a musical level, 'Fall Out' could be described as atypical of many punk records of the time: fast tempo, simplistic harmony and melody, apocalyptic lyrics and distorted guitar parts, not having any of the subtleties brought to the band by Andy Summers's guitar playing or, of course, Sting's songwriting. Its independent release was part of the trend set by other London-based labels such as Stiff and Chiswick, who, as outlined by Dave Laing, had proved that to release a record with 'only a few hundred pounds and not a vast bank loan' was possible.[42]

The gig at the Alexandria Club in Newport was the first date of a UK tour with Cherry Vanilla, in which the band went on to perform three nights in London (3, 4 and 6 March), and then consecutive nights in Warrington, Liverpool, Birmingham, Middlesbrough (9–12 March) and finally London and West Runton (15 and 17 March). These early UK performances during

March 1977 turned out to be the beginning of a period of touring, in which the band also supported Wayne County and The
Electric Chairs on a tour of the Netherlands between 19 and 27
March, followed by more work with Cherry Vanilla in the UK
between 3 April and 7 May.[43]

Considering the various newspaper adverts of these early
performances, it is interesting to note the gradual emergence of
The Police, both musically and as a brand. As already stated, the
name of the band itself was considered problematic at the first
performance in Newport. As she was the headline artist, it is not
surprising that Cherry Vanilla's American roots are highlighted
in newspaper adverts, with the performance at the Nag's Head
on 4 March 1977 described as 'New York Rock Part Two' and that
at The Nashville Room on 6 March as 'From New York'. In both
instances, unsurprisingly, The Police are advertised in a far smaller
and lighter-shade font. During their tour of the Netherlands
with Wayne County, The Police are given greater presence for
the Tweede Exloërmond gig on 19 March. Although they were
'below' Cherry Vanilla and Wayne County on the list of performers, the font of the band name is given equal stature. This is also
the case at the 'punk rock festival' in Amsterdam, where they
performed on 25 March alongside Wayne County, Cherry Vanilla
and Johnny Thunders. After a gig at The Marquee in London
on 25 May supporting Wayne County, Sting and Copeland gave
what has become an iconic performance that was attended by
'over five thousand French Hippies' at the Circus Hippodrome, a
permanent circus-type venue in eastern Paris, on 28 May.[44] Named
Strontium 90 by ex-Gong bass player Mike Howlett, the band was
put together to perform at what was billed as a Gong reunion
concert.[45] In addition to Sting and Copeland, the line-up featured
Howlett himself as a second bass/guitar player, in addition to
a friend of his on guitar – Andy Summers. Although they only
performed a short set as part of what was a twelve-hour festival,

this performance was to represent the first event in which the members of the definitive line-up of The Police recorded and performed in front of an audience.[46] According to Sting, he was introduced to Andy Summers while visiting the studio in Mike Howlett's 'pleasant terraced house' in Acton, West London – not far from Ealing Television Studios.[47] The house that Sting is referring to is located at 137b Southfield Road, a first-floor semi-detached maisonette, which had a small recording studio placed in the top-floor loft conversion.

> It had proper stairs up to the loft, and it had a little window, and they [the previous occupants] had lined it all with varnished pine. I had heard somewhere that varnished wood was really bad for [studio] reflection, echo and sound, so I actually stripped the entire room – it became stripped pine.[48]

Howlett had converted this space into what he described as his 'little recording room', with a small advance obtained from Virgin Publishing and using the money to purchase a four-track recorder, some microphones and a small mixing desk. At that time, he was living with Sting's Virgin Records-based publisher, Carol Wilson, who had arranged Last Exit's demo sessions at Pathway, after seeing the band support Alan Price at Newcastle City Hall.

> I had been recording my own material and I approached Simon Draper, who is Richard Branson's cousin, at Virgin. Simon liked it. After attempting to play drums and sing myself, I decided to get Sting in on vocals. So he came around [to 137b Southfield Road] and learnt my songs.[49]

Although it is a minor detail, Andy Summers recalls meeting Sting, not at Howlett's home, but 'at a small studio in Swiss Cottage called Virtual Earth', where the majority of the

Strontium 90 recordings took place.[50] Considering it is over forty years since this meeting took place, it is understandable that there is some confusion about the details of the event. When Howlett was asked to provide his version of the circumstances that ultimately led to the formation of The Police, he commented:

> [Andy Summers] had been in Kevin Coyne's backing band, who had supported Gong on a tour in around 1973 or 1974. I bumped into him in the January of 1977 at Lady June's mansion flat in [Vale Court] Maida Vale.[51]

Off the back of this meeting, Howlett invited Summers to perform at the aforementioned Gong reunion concert with Strontium 90, in addition to playing on his Virgin-financed demo recording – both of which also featured Sting and Stewart Copeland.

> So he [Andy Summers] came round and learned some of the material in my little flat in Acton. They both [Summers and Sting] came there – but they learnt the songs *individually*.[52]

Regarding the later introduction of Stewart Copeland into the Strontium 90 project, Howlett recalled having a drummer lined up for the session – Chris Cutler from Henry Cow. When Cutler told Howlett he could not make it, Sting informed Howlett,

> oh I know a drummer, I have been doing some stuff with Stewart Copeland. So Sting brings Stewart to Virtual Earth. My understanding is that Sting, Andy and Stewart played together for the first time in Virtual Earth Studios.[53]

Howlett recalled using these sessions, which commenced on 17 May 1977, to prepare for the Gong reunion concert in Paris, in addition to recording demo material, which was to be used to secure a potential recording contract.

It appears that during the rehearsals with Howlett, Sting realized that Andy Summers was the missing link he and Copeland needed to complete the line-up of The Police:

> This is the kind of musician I could write for, the kind of musician I could entrust with my songs, who could inspire me, who could realize the music in my head, and although I don't say anything because we are in Mike's studio, this is exactly the kind of musician that the Police need.[54]

Summers was already an experienced musician by this point. Not only had he worked with countless UK artists, including The Soft Machine, Eric Burdon and The Animals, Kevin Ayers and Kevin Coyne, to name a few, but he had studied classical guitar at the University of California. 'It would have been difficult in 1977 to find a guitarist with a wider range of experience than Summers, making him perhaps the unlikeliest of candidates for membership of an up-and-coming punk group.'[55]

Twenty years later, in 1997, Howlett released an album that is a combination of selected performances from the concert in Paris and six studio tracks from the Virtual Earth Studio sessions. Entitled *Strontium 90: Police Academy*, the album includes a version of 'Visions of the Night' and, more importantly, a demo version of 'Every Little Thing She Does Is Magic', which was eventually recorded by The Police and released on *Ghost in the Machine* in 1981. Listening to the demo of 'Every Little Thing She Does Is Magic', it is worth noting that the vast majority of the arrangement is already in place, with Sting accompanying himself on guitar during the first verse, after which he is accompanied by a basic drum part. The demo includes a near-identical form and harmonic framework to the later version, including the key change into the bridge, confirming Sting's tendency to present complete songs to his band members. Although the voice is unmistakably Sting's, it is more vulnerable in tone, breaking up on occasion, which actually substantiates the lyric of the piece and its Latin-American rhythm. Considering when this piece was recorded, it is obviously at odds both lyrically and musically with the punk rock scene the band were attempting to infiltrate – this may be the reason its official release was delayed until 1981. Just prior to performing the song, in a TV broadcast of 1996, Sting discussed writing it in 1976, moving to London and it being 'the year of punk and the Sex Pistols and anarchy and aggressive music and aggressive lyrics – just to show you how in tune with the time I was'.[56] Commenting on its suitability for The Police, he stated,

> It wasn't appropriate for The Police's first few records. It was later I had the courage to say 'Let's try this' . . . It was done with a great deal of resistance from the other two.[57]

Interestingly, although all of the other tracks on the Strontium 90 album are either recorded live in Paris or at Virtual Earth Studios, 'Every Little Thing She Does Is Magic' was originally recorded at Mike Howlett's project studio in Acton.

'Visions of the Night' was eventually released as the B-side to 'Walking on the Moon' in the UK. Unlike the demo of 'Every Little Thing She Does Is Magic', this early version does capture the spirit of the time due to its clear punk rock influences. Once again, there are strong similarities with the later version, although the official version is more authentic in terms of its shorter duration, its 'eighth note' guitar parts in the verse and its more aggressive lead vocal style. One of three songs on the album which were recorded live at the concert in Paris, Sting's '3 O'Clock Shot' is not a title which appears in his later catalogue, although it is easy to spot the harmonic similarity to 'Be My Girl – Sally', from *Outlandos*

137b Southfield Road, where Sting recorded his demo of 'Every Little Thing She Does Is Magic'.

d'Amour. Lyrically, '3 O'Clock Shot' also uses very similar content to the old Last Exit and future Police song 'O My God' – a reappropriation technique which was also applied to the song 'So Lonely'. At the time of the Virtual Earth recording, Sting's only previous reference point would have been the original Last Exit version of the song, so this represents an early example of Sting taking the lyrics of what was then a mid-tempo, gospel-influenced song and updating it to a style which had more commercial potential and resonance with his new group. All of the other tracks on the album were composed by Howlett and, listening to them separately, they appear to have a greater musical tendency towards the music that punk was replacing, requiring more technical proficiency, being more musically complex and having overt acid rock influences.[58] Howlett initially considered releasing the album on his own label after he had a number of fans 'pestering [him] to put it out'.

After speaking to Sting ten years previously, when a band he was producing (Berlin) were supporting The Police at Hollywood Park, and then again in the early '90s at the Ivor Novello Awards, Howlett was given informal permission to proceed with the project. Andy Summers and Stewart Copeland also gave the project their go-ahead. Despite these informal green lights, Howlett then experienced a period in which he struggled with Sting's management to agree suitable terms for the release. Eventually *Strontium 90: Police Academy* was released on Sting's label, Pangea.

During the recording of the Strontium 90 album, Sting was the only member of the band not to have international credentials, his only previous work being at a local level. It is obvious, however, that the years spent paying his dues in Newcastle had served him well, as he is not out of his depth musically in these early recordings. Upon reflection, this album represents an interesting example of Sting and The Police in transition, as they are halfway between the jazz/progressive rock background of the musicians involved and the punk/new wave influences The Police would go on to explore more in the months ahead. Indeed, considering the technical capacity of all four performers, it could be argued that they were consciously holding back their technical abilities in order to comply with the emerging new style.[59]

Asked about how the members of Strontium 90 resonated with the punk movement, Howlett explained how his partner Carol Wilson had been given an early pressing of *Never Mind the Bollocks, Here's the Sex Pistols* album in late 1976/early 1977 and how it prompted him to change one of the songs from a rock ballad to double the tempo. 'I was aware that there was a sea change in music and what that represented.' He also recalled the audience at the Paris concert thinking that the band were 'pure punk, because we came on as hard hitting [and] speedy'.[60]

The original line-up of The Police continued supporting Cherry Vanilla up until 12 May 1977; that month culminated in the

aforementioned performance at the Circus Hippodrome. After
returning from Paris, they started a series of ten consecutive gigs
in London over a two-month period, during which they began to
be the headline act. The first performance was on 31 May 1977, in
what was described as a 'New Wave Night' at the Railway Hotel in
Putney, followed by gigs at venues such as The Marquee on 4 and
24 June, The Roxy on 10 and 17 June, and the Hope and Anchor
on 8 July, the last two venues in particular being synonymous with
the emerging punk scene in London. Throughout 1977, the Hope
and Anchor pub served as a regular venue for emerging punk and
what were being described as new wave bands. The venue was
frequented by artists such as The Stranglers, who recorded their
Live at the Hope and Anchor there in November 1977 as part of the
Front Row Festival. This festival itself spurred a double live album,
the *Hope & Anchor Front Row Festival* (1978), which featured pub rock
artists, such as Wilko Johnson and Dire Straits; punk/new wave
bands, such as XTC and 999; and Steel Pulse – the only instance of
a reggae band. The venue was also used in the film *Breaking Glass*
from 1980, featuring Hazel O'Connor in the story of an emerging
new wave band.

 Commencing its short-lived existence with three consecutive
gigs by Generation X, Johnny Thunders and Siouxsie and the
Banshees in December 1976, The Roxy in Covent Garden was also
an iconic venue in the development of the British punk movement.
Released in July 1977, around nine months prior to the live album
recorded at the Hope and Anchor, *Live at the Roxy wc2* featured artists such as Slaughter and the Dogs, Wire, X-Ray Spex, Buzzcocks
and The Adverts, all of whom played at the venue during its first
few months in business.[61] The Adverts ex-member T. V. Smith (Tim
Smith) recalled it not being the 'location that counted':

> it was the congregation that gave it significance. Hundreds
> of us hungry for stimulation and the chance to share the

excitement of this growing scene would troop on a regular basis down the narrow stairway into the dingy basement of the Roxy eager to see what tonight's bunch of ragged hopefuls had for us.[62]

Around two months after the Gong reunion performance, Sting, Copeland, Howlett and Summers performed again at Dingwalls on 12 July 1977, followed closely by a gig at The Nashville Room in London on 21 July – this time they were called The Elevators, the name change being the result of Strontium 90 being too 'esoteric', according to Howlett.[63] However, despite

Sting, Copeland and Padavani sitting outside The Roxy in London in June 1977.

the new name and Howlett's attempt to bring new energy to the project, Sting and Copeland came to the conclusion 'that this particular lift [sic] isn't going to get off the floor'.[64]

After a sensitive personal process, in which both Howlett and Padovani were diplomatically ousted from their respective bands, the first performance of The Police with Andy Summers took place at Rebecca's in Birmingham, on 18 August 1977; the performance was incorrectly dated as the day that Elvis Presley died in Andy Summers's autobiography. This was preceded by two gigs featuring both Summers and Padovani, the first at The Music Machine in London on 25 July and the second at Mont-de-Marsan in France on 5 August. After these gigs, The Police returned to Pathway Studios, once again with both Padovani and Andy Summers, on 10 August 1977, to record 'Dead End Job' plus two takes of 'Visions of the Night', which were subsequently combined and released on the aforementioned B-side to 'Walking on the Moon' in the UK.[65] It is, to date, the only studio recording to feature all four members of The Police performing simultaneously.

Situated in Severn Street Birmingham, Rebecca's is described by Sting in his autobiography as 'a small nightclub/discotheque', remembering the venue as the place where he realised he now had a 'flagship for [his] songs'.[66] The reason for this new-found confidence was the guitar playing of Andy Summers; Summers recalls the planned hour-long set being 'done in twelve minutes' at the venue.[67] Though Summers likened the performance to the music of Dizzy Gillespie and Charlie Parker in the 1940s in terms of intensity, he regarded the event as 'pitiful', being 'so intent on being viewed as punk that [they] miss[ed] the music entirely'.[68] Mike Howlett, who saw the band a few days later, had a similar perspective to Summers, believing 'They [The Police] were trying to be punk. They played everything super fast, but unfortunately super tight. Except for Henry [Padovani] who was

a true punk, it was somehow bogus. You could tell it was not
honest music.'[69] Comparing the early gigs of The Police with
those of Last Exit, Phil Sutcliffe agreed with these perspectives:

> Looking at the two bands, The Police were dreadful at what
> they did to start with and Last Exit were very good at what
> they did. [However], The Police were dreadful within a fash-
> ion, [while] Last Exit were good with no fashion to support
> them . . . I am sure to some degree that influenced Sting's
> decision [to leave Last Exit], although I am sure he would still
> say – he loved the sort of music Last Exit were playing.[70]

One of a number of clubs and venues owned by the
Birmingham-based Fewtrell family, Rebecca's was spread over three
floors named the Casaba, the Blue Soul Room and the Sin Bin, the
latter of which was in the basement.[71] The venue was opened in
1966, named after Edward Fewtrell's daughter. Examining similar
gigs that took place at the venue just prior to the performance by
The Police, artists included Blondie, The Jam and XTC, and like the
earlier performances of The Police, the event was labelled 'new
wave', as opposed to punk, in order to abate the public's concern
regarding the negative connotations of the latter.[72]

In terms of the London-based performances by The Police
after Andy Summers joined the band, according to Sting's website, in the fourteen-month period between 18 August 1977 and
3 October 1978, The Police performed in London eleven times,
including a performance at The Rock Garden, two performances
at The Marquee, two performances at The Nashville Room, one
performance at Rochester Castle and two performances at the
Hope and Anchor. The majority of these gigs took place between
22 January and 23 April 1978, during which time there were only
two performances outside London, at Essex University and at the
Locarno Ballroom in Bristol.

What used to be the main entrance to Rebecca's in Birmingham: the first venue in which the definitive line-up of The Police performed together.

A rare performance outside of London: The Police pictured just prior to their performance at the Locarno Ballroom in Bristol on 12 March 1978.

Although the first set of London performances with Padovani was interspersed with European gigs, this second set of concerts was followed by an initial visit to his eventual home, New York – at CBGBS on 20 October 1978. These concerts represent a time through which the band began the process of slowly developing their musical identity, gradually becoming distinct from the punk movement that inspired their formation. Although they continued to perform in England's capital, their momentum towards becoming a world band had started, performing far less frequently after October 1978 – eleven times in 1979, twice in 1980 and three times in 1981. Sting had made his first steps towards being a global superstar.

6 SONGWRITING

Now living in the capital of England, Sting continued his use of independent recording studios. Having used Impulse, Pathway and Virtual Earth, the first two albums by The Police were to be recorded at Surrey Sound in Leatherhead, his last significant use of a small independent studio. So as a northern jazz rock musician living in London at the apex of the punk rock movement, Sting began the process of making sense of his past, while also looking for opportunities to understand how to use all of his experiences as the processes and products of his creativity.

After moving to London, Sting lived in a number of temporary accommodations throughout his first few years in the capital. According to his autobiography, he and his young family initially stayed at a friend's flat on Prince of Wales Drive in Battersea, 'taking over the sitting room until we can find a place of our own to rent'.[1] This was followed by the process of finding their own permanent home.

> You spend hours driving across London only to find that the flat has already been let or that you would have to share your Dickensian accommodations with a family of rodents, and all the cars in the street are vandalized wrecks.[2]

After having been disappointed while trying to secure a flat in Southgate, when the owners decided they did not want an unemployed musician as a tenant, Sting and his family had the

An early photo of the definitive line-up of The Police, outside Sting's flat in Bayswater Road, London.

opportunity to sublet an 'elegant terraced house in Bark Place off the Bayswater Road'.[3] Although it was only temporary accommodation, Sting remembers the house fondly:

> The house had belonged to a Lord and Lady Dunnet . . . [and had] large spacious rooms on four floors, filled with sculptures and paintings . . . The main room downstairs had a grand piano . . . This is probably the grandest place I've lived in until now.[4]

This was followed by what was to be his first 'permanent' accommodation in the capital, a housing association basement flat at 28 Leinster Square, also in Bayswater. It was in this home that Sting composed some early songs by The Police, in addition to meeting his second wife, Trudie Styler, who lived at number 32.[5]

I'd drive back to London in my battered old Citroën . . .
with these songs thundering in my head, yelling improvised
lyrics at the top of my voice . . . I'd get back to my flat in
Bayswater . . . I'd try to scribble down whatever I'd been
declaiming in the car and then go to sleep . . . The afternoon
would be spent trying to make sense of these fragments and
working on them until early evening so that I would have
something presentable that night.[6]

If one looks back on the lead-in to Sting moving to London, there
can be no doubt that the contacts and sheer persistence of his
wife, Frances Tomelty, had a positive impact on his early career.
In the twelve months leading up to his departure from Newcastle,
Sting recalls Tomelty

effectively [becoming] our [Last Exit's] manager . . . turning
our efforts into a whirlwind of activity on our behalf. She calls
every major record company in London and arranges meetings with the A and R departments . . . she uses her engaging
charm and considerable presence to get through the doors of
Island Records, Chrysalis, Pye, Charisma, Virgin, EMI, A&M,
Arista, Decca, as well as booking agents, while also sending
tapes to pubs and clubs around the metropolis.[7]

Soon after moving to London with Sting, Tomelty was obtaining
regular work as an actress, and was also able indirectly to secure
him some modelling work via her agent friend Pippa Markham.
For example, in early 1978, Sting appeared in TV adverts for
Wrigley's Spearmint Gum, Triumph Bras and Brutus Jeans.
Although never aired, the Wrigley's advert involved all members
of The Police and, according to Christopher Sandford, was
the reason behind the dyed blond hair adopted by the group.
Sandford dates the making of this advert to 22 February 1978,

marking an inadvertent move towards the band's now-famous blond-haired image.[8] The uniform haircuts of a pop group were, of course, not a new phenomenon, The Beatles being the most famous example during the 1960s, and the style was also incorporated loosely by contemporary late-1970s bands such as The Jam and The Ramones.

Just prior to the Wrigley's advert and soon after performing a Last Exit reunion concert at Newcastle's University Theatre Bar, Sting returned to London and began recording the first album by The Police, *Outlandos d'Amour*. Recording commenced in January 1978 at Surrey Sound Studios in Leatherhead and, according to Sting, was completed in ten days 'for less than fifteen hundred pounds'.[9] Andy Summers remembers the sessions as more drawn-out, taking place 'over a period of about six months, borrowing days and jumping in when other people's sessions are cancelled'.[10] This does not negate Sting's account, but clarifies that the 'ten days' took place in January, with the remainder of the sessions

Frances Tomelty and baby son Joe, outside their basement flat in Bayswater, *c.* 1977.

The Police in Sting's basement flat in Bayswater, with Sting and Stewart Copeland's dyed blond hair.

taking place over the coming months, in a similar fashion to the deal Last Exit had with Impulse Sound Recording Studio, only a few years previously.

The Police performed in London eight times between 12 January and 23 April 1978, and as these performances were the means through which all members of the band made their living, additional work had to be found, since there was no record company advance for recording their debut album. Therefore, in addition to the abovementioned commercial work, Sting undertook a few minor film roles. According to his autobiography, this work commenced in 'the late summer of 1978', with a small part in the Sex Pistols' *The Great Rock 'n' Roll Swindle*, although Sting's scene was ultimately cut from the movie by the time it was released in 1980.[11] It was, however, reintroduced in *The Filth and the Fury* (2000), largely comprising archive footage from the original movie, in which Sting can be seen playing the part of a member of fictional gay band The Blow Waves, kidnapping the Sex Pistols' drummer Paul Jones. Sting also acquired a role in the 'road movie' *Radio On*, in which he plays a guitar-playing garage attendant who performs Eddie Cochran's 'Three Steps to Heaven' on a semi-acoustic guitar. A few months prior to this, Sting secured the part of Ace Face in *Quadrophenia*, in the summer of 1978, when the band were just becoming known. By the time of its release in August 1979, The Police were becoming a force in the music industry, headlining at the Reading Festival on 24 August 1979 and having top-twenty hits with 'Roxanne' and 'Can't Stand Losing You' and success with *Outlandos d'Amour*, which peaked at number six in April 1979 in the UK.[12] Upon examination of the culmination of factors that took place leading into the summer of 1979, it is apparent that the publicity around *Quadrophenia*, a movie that Sting originally undertook simply to subsidize his music-based income, had a positive impact on the success of The Police.[13] According to Andy Summers, 'With *Quadrophenia* our name is everywhere and we surge forward like a Viking ship, with Sting as the bowsprit [*sic*].'[14] Returning to the recording of their debut album, Surrey Sound was originally built as a four-track studio in 1975 by brothers Nigel and Chris Gray, and considered 'no more salubrious than Pathway' by Sting, despite the fact that it had been upgraded to a sixteen-track Alice desk and Ampex MM1000 sixteen-track machine by the time The Police recorded their first album.[15] Sting was probably referring to the limited space in the studio, the sloped ceiling in the live room of which was apparently used to positive effect by Stewart Copeland to obtain greater variety of drum sound.[16] A more inadvertent impact of the space can also be heard in 'Roxanne', when Sting accidentally leaned against an upright piano at the start of the song, a 'mistake' the band decided to keep. Owner Nigel Gray produced the first album and also the subsequent two, although by the time The Police recorded *Reggatta de Blanc* in 1979, the studio had been upgraded to a 24-track MCI machine.

Despite the fact that this was Sting's first album and that he considered himself 'a novice in terms of recording' experience, all of the songs on *Outlandos d'Amour* were composed or co-written by him – while on tour, in the car, during rehearsals and recording sessions, at home, or with his previous band Last Exit.[17] This was a pattern that would continue throughout the lifespan of The Police, resulting not only in ill feeling between the members, but significant differences in earning power.[18] Subject matters of the first album ranged from historical incidents (for example, 'Born in the '50s') to the loneliness of missing his wife. Interestingly, six of the songs are love songs in the broadest sense of the term: 'So Lonely', 'Next to You', 'Roxanne', 'Hole in my Life', 'Can't Stand Losing You' and 'Be My Girl – Sally'. Some of these songs provide a snapshot of Sting's state of mind at the time.

'Next to You' seems to address Sting's experiences of living so far away from his wife Frances Tomelty – who only several months earlier was based in London while he was still in Newcastle. Aside from the repeated refrain in the chorus, which speaks for itself, the song broadly discusses how the protagonist needs to leave where s/he is living. Sting is, of course, talking about his need to leave Newcastle and relocate to London, so the song represents this transition – even if it may have been retrospective.[19] It is interesting to compare this song with The Animals' 'We Gotta Get Out of this Place' (1965), which deals with a similar subject. Although the song was written by Brill Building composers Barry Mann and Cynthia Weil, with an American sensibility, The Animals' version had obvious allusions to Newcastle, with lines outlining the 'dirty city' and the need to escape having clear resonances. Both of these songs, of course, are associated not just with a specific place, but with a more universal feeling of escaping. Asked about Sting's complex relationship with Newcastle and his early need to 'escape', Phil Sutcliffe made the following observation about the song:

> Sting's thing [complex relationship with his hometown] goes back before music and all that. It goes back to the sense of himself as figuring out how intelligent he was, figuring out what he might be capable of [and] that buffeting against what his life was predicting for him.[20]

Sutcliffe then made a connection between Sting's background and that of his friend Bruce Springsteen. When asked if they were similar, he commented,

> 'We Gotta Get Out of This Place' was one of the key tracks of Springsteen's teens. So he is listening to a Geordie, singing a song . . . That song is written by a couple of people from the Brill Building, but it sounds as though it was written in Newcastle [and it] sounds as though it was written in New Jersey – and it hit those two guys. [Like Sting's], Springsteen's parents had a dysfunctional relationship . . . I am sure that is why when they went on the Amnesty Tour they hit it off. They spent a lot of time together then, and they are still friends. 'We Gotta Get Out of This Place' is such a significant song for both of them – the place is both literal and metaphorical.[21]

The lyrics of 'So Lonely' were written originally for the Last Exit song 'Fool in Love', thus inadvertently referencing Sting's time in Newcastle. In his *Lyrics by Sting* book, Sting discusses how he 'grafted them [the lyrics] shamelessly onto the chords from Bob Marley's 'No Woman, No Cry' and how the contrasting rock and roll chorus 'pleased the hell' out of him.[22] Like the other love-based songs on *Outlandos d'Amour*, the lyrics resonate very strongly with Sting's displeasure at being apart from Frances Tomelty, on this occasion once again commenting on the logistics of him being based in Newcastle while she was in London.

Sting's image developing: on the stairs leading to his basement flat in Bayswater.

Sandford regarded the personal nature of some of the songs on *Outlandos d'Amour* as 'reading as though they'd come straight from [Sting's] diary', although also very much a collaboration between the members of the group, with 'Copeland and Summers [having been responsible for] embellishing the basic tunes'.[23] Andy Summers remembers the album as 'ultimately [being the] distillation of about three albums . . . We recognise flaws and imperfections and begin the process of abandoning songs and writing new ones.'[24] Regarding the ways in which Sting's songs were 'embellished', Summers commented,

> Over the top of these patterns [Sting's reggae-influenced bass lines], I begin playing high, cloudy chords that are coloured by echo and delay, and Stewart counters this with back-to-front patterns on the hi-hat and snare. From a dense in-your-face frontal assault, the songs now become filled with air and light.[25]

In terms of the compositional process employed by The Police, the ideas behind the groove and texture of the first album were very much a joint effort, in which Sting effectively used the rehearsal process as a compositional tool. Regarding the groove of 'Roxanne', for example, he discussed how the song evolved 'into a hybrid tango through trial-and-error . . . It is Stewart who suggests stressing the second beat of each bar on the bass and bass drum, giving the song its lopsided Argentinian gait.'[26] Although he considered the resultant style to be reggae as opposed to tango, Andy Summers recalled the original style being in a bossa nova rhythm and, while conceding that the rhythm 'worked', he believed that 'in the prevailing [music industry] climate it would be suicidal to go Brazilian':

> So how should we play it? . . . We decide to try it with a reggae rhythm, at which point Stewart starts to play a sort

of backward hi-hat and tells Sting where to put the bass hits. Once the bass and drums are in place, the right counterpoint for me to play is the four in the bar rhythm part.[27]

Sting's working methods can be regarded as typical of rock music in terms of the way in which he introduced songs to his fellow band members – by bringing sketches to a rehearsal and allowing the band to flesh out the arrangement. However, this is not the way Sting had always worked, nor how he would necessarily work with musicians in the future. Although former Last Exit guitarist John Hedley remembers rehearsals at the Gosforth Hotel in Newcastle as being informal, 'with all members contributing some material', keyboardist Gerry Richardson recalls the leadership of the band gradually moving from his to Sting's direction as the years progressed.[28]

Several years later, Hedley recalled visiting Sting's flat in Bayswater and listening to what sounded like a complete demo of 'Walking on the Moon', with all parts played by Sting on a multi-track tape recorder. (Hedley is probably referring to the use of what Sting refers to as 'Dennis the drum box' in the BBC production *Police in Montserrat*.) Filmed during the making of their fourth album *Ghost in the Machine*, Sting recalls writing parts of 'Message in a Bottle' in the back of a bus, using a Sony tape recorder with a built-in drum machine to document his ideas.[29] So by the early '80s, Sting's songs were compiled in fragments over time, on the road, and sometimes recorded in demo format, often with the aid of technology, and then presented to his fellow band members after he had 'joined all the different bits of tape together'.[30] After the song was presented to the band members, they got the opportunity to 'learn it . . . adapt it and change it'.[31] However, by the time The Police were recording *Ghost in the Machine*, he had not only continued his dominance as the band's songwriter, but had also begun to take control of the arrangement process, leaving less space for his fellow band members to utilize their own creativity:

> Sting doesn't bring in half-finished songs anymore. His ideas are brilliant, but more and more we're stuck with them, and he's liking it less and less when we mess with them.[32]

Regarding 'Every Little Thing She Does Is Magic', Andy Summers recalls the band using 'Sting's expensive demo as the actual track [that ended up on the final album]; Stewart and I just have to try and fit ourselves into it.'[33] This resulted in not only creative frustration, but ill feeling, with Summers commenting 'most of my songwriting . . . comes to nothing'.[34]

Presenting 'complete' ideas to band members was not new for Sting. Discussing the Last Exit demo recordings he made with Sting during the mid-1970s, Gerry Richardson commented,

> Just about everything in all those songs, you know there may be something in the drum groove, but he [Sting] has come up with the bass line, he would usually come up with the guitar parts as well . . . Nearly all the guitar parts of The Police are [composed by] Sting . . . His hand size – you know the arpeggio on 'Every Breath You Take'? Sting's got huge hands . . . I can recall John Hedley telling me Andy Summers [was] struggling like hell to play that arpeggio.[35]

Asked about how he presented songs to his fellow band members during the mid-1970s, Richardson continued,

> He always writes complete versions of songs . . . I mean fully composed lyrics, bass lines . . . A lot of the keyboard parts are mine – but that riff on [the Last Exit version of] 'I Burn For You' is Sting. You know that repetitive two handed figure? It's

always been the same way, Last Exit, The Police, then through to Sting's own band, he's a composer *and* arranger. There are certain things that other people have contributed to, but generally most of the parts come from him.[36]

As opposed to getting into the technical details of who composed what in the recordings of The Police, it is arguably more interesting to take a closer look at Sting's songwriting processes. This can be done by listening to interviews and early recordings of songs, but that paints only a partial picture. It is also useful to regard the songwriting process as a form of knowledge-based problem solving, in which the writer is simply finding solutions to musical problems:

> problem solvers begin with some basic material, the starting state, and some desired solution, the goal state. They then make a series of choices that transforms the starting state into the goal state.[37]

Sting uses a sort of cut and paste technique to join various musical ideas together, either by updating older ideas and annotating them onto paper or portable recording technology, or by using the band as a compositional tool. However, where do Sting's initial ideas come from and how does he solve his musical problems? Regarding the inspiration behind his lyrics and harmony, he commented,

> Normally I write the music first. It doesn't matter if it's a tune or a series of chords . . . I'll construct a song entirely without lyrics. My theory is that music, when it's structured correctly, has a narrative. It's an abstract narrative but it's nonetheless a story: beginning, a bridge, a key change, coda . . . So it's my job to translate that narrative into

something that people will recognise as a story. Most of my songs are written that way.[38]

He then provides an insight into one technique he uses to develop the song:

I take the music away when it's finished. I put it in an iPod and go for a walk and I free-associate and usually come back with something that I can recognize as an end point of the story. Then I say, 'so how do I get to that?'[39]

Using the song 'I Hung My Head' as an example, Sting continues,

It started with a walk in the country thinking 'what is this song about, what is the narrative telling me?' It's a kind of Western. It sounded like a horse, a lame horse, the rhythm of it was strange.[40]

Having come up with the refrain 'I Hung My Head', he then asked himself a number of questions to develop the detailed lyrical content:

but what does that mean? Why would that be? What sort of person would say that? What kind of situation would he be in? So I write the story backwards.[41]

Based on the comments above, it is possible to consider Sting as initially using what are essentially abstract musical ideas and giving linguistic meaning to them – in much the same way a movie composer equates sound to a moving image. When making these early creative decisions, which appear to resonate with a problem-solving approach, he is obviously of the opinion that *music on its own* (without lyrics) has meaning *beyond* its sound textures, making it possible to marry the sound and lyrics together in a symbiotic union. Sting takes this relationship a stage further, by juxtaposing lyrical content that resonates *against* its musical backing. As mentioned previously, this can include simply positioning 'sad' lyrical content against 'happy-sounding' music – the chorus of 'So Lonely' is an excellent example of this. This tendency can also be heard throughout the first two albums on songs such as 'Next to You', 'Hole in My Life', 'Can't Stand Losing You' and 'The Bed's too Big without You'. Discussing a later song, 'King of Pain', Sting commented, 'this song has made me famous for writing really depressing lyrics over a really jolly tune.'[42]

Looking at musical inspiration, composer Jonathan Harvey considers it 'to be defined as that which causes, provokes, [or] forces the artist to create – [it is] the catalyst of the creative process.'[43] Labelling it 'the hidden cause', Harvey continues to suggest that inspiration is more difficult to describe than to identify:

> It may be almost impossible for the listener to pinpoint its presence . . . yet without it the work would not have the individuality for which, presumably, we admire it.[44]

On one level, it can be relatively straightforward to *understand* why Sting has made particular creative decisions. For example, by considering his social background, it is not difficult to suggest reasons why he wrote about topics such as the miners' strike in 'We Work the Black Seam' or composed a Broadway production loosely based on the shipbuilding town of Wallsend. It is also easy to understand why he dedicated . . . *Nothing Like the Sun* and *The Soul Cages* to his parents after their respective deaths, considering the complex relationship he had with them. Likewise, regarding the punk and reggae influences of his songwriting in the early years of The Police, it is fair to suggest that these decisions were simply based on what was happening in the underground scene in

London, at the time he moved there. It is also possible to consider the allusions to classical literature in his music as an indicator of either his grammar school upbringing or his intention to distance himself from his working-class roots, or a mixture of both. In addition to incorporating this device in his solo career, with album titles such as *Ten Summoner's Tales*,[45] it can also be traced in some songs by The Police, such as 'Bring on the Night', 'Don't Stand So Close to Me', 'Secret Journey' and 'Tea in the Sahara'.[46] It is even possible to propose that some of Sting's songs are simply inspired by his life circumstances at the time: his love life, travelling, where he was living, what he watched on the news, his politics, the Bible – not to mention the titles of the last two albums by The Police, *Ghost in The Machine* and *Synchronicity*, which were influenced by Arthur Koestler's 1967 book *The Ghost in the Machine* and his later work *The Roots of Coincidence* of 1972, which made reference to Carl Jung's philosophical concept of Synchronicity.[47]

In a similar fashion, the shift in Sting's less-than-democratic working methods can be put down to his rising status as a rock star, increased confidence / ego or indeed his ability to use portable recording technology to generate ideas that may previously have required a band. None of these suggestions, however, helps us fully to understand the 'creative spark' that instigates his songs – the 'hidden cause' that Jonathan Harvey mentions above. Considering his musical inspiration, Sting discussed practicalities such as daily practice to 'keep the muscle going' and simply investing time in his craft: 'I don't think we compose so much as we just find things. Collate them.'[48] He proceeds to discuss how inspiration is 'largely an unconscious process', in which the songwriter needs to 'get into a state where you allow things to come through'.[49]

> Which begs the question: are you writing anything or is it being written for you in some other, collective unconscious-ness? I don't know the answer to that.[50]

Sting is obviously referencing the long-standing influence he
drew from the works of Carl Jung, who famously wrote about
the 'collective unconsciousness' and whose terminology to
describe it became the name of the final album by The Police –
Synchronicity.[51] Sting gets into the compositional state he refers to
through activities such as walking or practising yoga, although he
confesses the ideas often occur unexpectedly:

> I was lying in bed in a hotel room in Munich, with this boom
> ba boom bass line running in my head. I scribbled the rhythm
> down in my notebook, guessing at the notes . . . hoping I
> would be able to make sense of my hieroglyphics the next
> morning.[52]

Sting is referring to the initial creative spark that was to become
'Walking on the Moon'. In another article, he refers to the phrase
'walking round the room' being the lyrical starting point of the
song – which was subsequently changed to its now-famous title.

> Walking on the Moon seemed a useful metaphor for being
> in love, that feeling of lightness or just being able to walk on
> air . . . So from that refrain I just worked backwards, so 1969:
> giant steps are what you take, one giant step for mankind . . .
> It's not meant to be serious.[53]

Sting has suffered from two lengthy periods of writer's block
during his career – initially in the early 1990s, and then once again
in the ten-year period prior to composing *The Last Ship* in 2013.
Attempting to explain this sudden reduction in inspiration, he
commented,

> So you start asking yourself questions. What have I done to
> offend the gods that they would abandon me so? Is the gift

of songwriting taken away as easily as it seems to have been bestowed?[54]

He then questions if there is 'a deeper physiological reason' behind his lack of ideas:

There was always a Faustian pact anyway. You're rewarded for revealing your innermost thoughts. Your private emotions on the page for the entertainment of others.[55]

This is followed by Sting describing the moment that instigated the return of his inspiration:

Perhaps you've given enough of your privacy away. And yet, if you look at your work, could it be argued that your best work wasn't about you at all? It was about somebody else. Does your best work occur when you've sidestepped your own ego, and you stop telling your story and you start telling someone else's story? Someone perhaps without a voice?[56]

After asking himself the question 'if you can't write about yourself anymore who do you write about', he comments on how returning to his hometown was once again the answer to his writer's block.

It's ironic that the landscape you have worked so hard to escape and the community I had more or less abandoned and exiled myself from, should be the very landscape, the very community I would have to return to, to find my missing muse . . . As soon as I decided to honour the community I came from . . . the songs started to come thick and fast. I have described it as a kind of projectile vomiting . . . Entire songs,

almost formed whole in front of me, as if they had been
bundled up inside of me for many, many years.[57]

With these comments, Sting is alluding to the profound and
often-complex nature of not only his own musical inspiration, but
also that of others. Tchaikovsky, for example, seems to differentiate
between the 'part of his brain' that engages with music and his
unconscious inspiration, resulting in 'a work composed in the
happiest surroundings [being] touched with dark and gloomy
colours'.[58] Sting's comment above regarding music being 'written in
some other collective unconsciousness' has resonance with composers such as Igor Stravinsky: 'I am the vessel through which *Le Sacre*
passed'; Gustav Mahler: 'One is, so to speak, only an instrument on
which the whole universe plays'; and Jean Sibelius: 'The power driving us [the composer] is that marvellous logic which governs a work
of art. Let us call it God.'[59] Although Sting is an atheist, perhaps

The World Unicorn at the bottom of Leslie Street, Wallsend, in 1973, in close proximity to
Sting's house in Gerald Street. It was images such as these that inspired *The Last Ship* (2013).

most famously outlined in his song 'O My God', there is certainly a spiritual aspect to some of his later work in particular. The entirety of *Sacred Love*, for example, falls into this category, many of the tracks dealing with the concept of love, and on occasion referencing the Bible. Interestingly, Sting deals with both the positives of love in songs such as 'Send Your Love', which encourages the listener to 'send your love into the future', and its complexities in songs such as 'Inside'. Listening to these tracks and others on *Sacred Love*, the multidimensional representation of love gives the listener a holistic perspective of what the word means – it is important to understand what it is not in order to comprehend what it is. Love, of course, is the single greatest command in the Christian Bible, with the eponymously named title track 'Sacred Love' referencing the book of Genesis on numerous occasions, in addition to the book of Deuteronomy. Also, the song 'Dead Man's Rope' quotes Sting's own 'Walking in Your Footsteps' towards the end, but somehow positions it within a Christian context, with the protagonist of the song progressing from walking away *in* emptiness and sorrow, to walking away *from* emptiness and sorrow. Like 'Fragile' and 'Every Breath You Take', this appears to be another example of a song in which Sting facilitates listeners to populate it with their own mean- ing – even if this is distinct from his own beliefs.

Although it could be argued that songs enabling listeners to hear their own personal life stories played out are the basis of much widely disseminated popular music, Sting is also well known for writing songs that have a specific message, in which he intends the meaning to be very clear. Always considering himself a socialist, Sting's interest in political song slowly began to emerge as he approached the end of his tenure with The Police, becoming an important part of his early solo career.

7 POLITICS

Despite his wealth, Sting has always described himself as a musician with strong socialist tendencies. Although many could argue
that extreme wealth makes this position difficult to defend, what
celebrity offers is a public voice. This is something that Sting used
to great effect in the 1980s, not only in his music, but via participa-
tion in live events such as Live Aid, his overt support for Amnesty
International and, of course, the establishment of his own charity
– The Rainforest Foundation. These activities received much
criticism in the national press, however, raising the question, are
political events populated by rock stars genuine, or simply a form
of cheap publicity?

   While Sting's early recordings tended to focus mainly on
autobiographical subjects – what one music journalist unfairly
described as 'songs that any twelve-year-old could sing and
understand' – his political stance began to emerge gradually
while he was still with The Police, with songs such as 'Driven to
Tears', 'Spirits in the Material World', 'Rehumanize Yourself' and
'One World (Not Three)', commenting on the world's lack of
awareness of 'the images of horror', its need for higher (spiritual)
awareness, local news that concerned him and Third World
issues.[1] Although the final album by The Police, *Synchronicity*, like
its predecessor *Ghost in the Machine,* was heavily influenced by the
writings of Arthur Koestler, it did not continue with any overt
political content, tending to be more intellectual, reflective and

Raising money for a hospital in Nigeria: people wait at the start of the Oxfam Walk with their entry forms on 5 May 1967, with a young Sting in the centre of picture.

philosophical. However, a moral imperative to use his celebrity status to 'educate the world' still appeared to be looming large. Having written the album in the luxurious surroundings at Goldeneye (James Bond creator Ian Fleming's old house, just outside the small town of Oracabessa on Jamaica's north coast), Sting commented,

> Britain had gone to war with Argentina over the Falklands. Young men were dying in the freezing waters of the South Atlantic, while I was gazing at sunspots on a cliff top over-looking the Caribbean.[2]

Although omitted from the vinyl version of *Synchronicity*, the song 'Murder by Numbers' (the B-side of 'Every Breath You Take' and included in later CD versions of the album) did include overt political comment. A mid-tempo jazz-influenced piece on the surface, its cutting lyrics come to their pinnacle towards the end, with Sting commenting on how 'you can reach the top of your profession' by becoming the 'leader of the land' and how 'murder is the sport of the elected', although 'you don't need to lift a finger of your hand'.[3] Despite the fact that no one is mentioned by name, the 'you' of the song is clearly aimed at politicians, Sting's earlier guilt-ridden comments regarding the 'young men of war' possibly having been an inspiration.

According to Sting, controversial televangelist Jimmy Swaggart described the song as 'an example of the devil's work'.[4] The Police were, in fact, not the only popular music band to engage with Swaggart: Bob Dylan recorded 'Disease of Conceit' (*Oh Mercy*, 1989), and Frank Zappa referred to Swaggart's widely publicized sex scandal in a number of his recordings, most famously *The Best Band You Never Heard in Your Life* (1991) and *Broadway the Hard Way* (1988). The latter is particularly interest-ing, as it includes a guest appearance from Sting, who performs

'Murder by Numbers' with Zappa's band. Although Sting had never met Zappa before this impromptu live performance, he was named in Zappa's autobiography as being one of the few famous artists to back Zappa's 'voter registration' initiative aimed at encouraging young Americans to use their vote by setting up polling stations at concerts.[5] At some performances, Sting would tactfully describe the song as being about the manipulation of large groups of people, a comment that also had an ironic resonance with Zappa, who sometimes playfully criticized his audiences for being aimlessly influenced by politicians and the media.

We will return to Sting's solo career political recordings later. On the subject of live performances, following his role in the Band Aid recording 'Do They Know It's Christmas' of 1984 and the subsequent Live Aid concert the following year at Wembley Stadium, in 1986 – alongside U2, Peter Gabriel, Joan Baez, The Neville Brothers and Bryan Adams – Sting participated in a tour celebrating the 25th anniversary of Amnesty International. Entitled 'Conspiracy of Hope', its aim was to raise not only funds, but *awareness* of human rights issues. The six-date tour became the first of what was to be known collectively as 'The Human Rights Concerts', a total of 28 performances featuring numerous artists and taking place between 1986 and 1998. Organized by the u.s. division of Amnesty International, the performances were, in fact, influenced by what became known as The Secret Policeman's Ball, a series of comedy events that started in 1976 in the uk. These events began to include music in the late 1970s – Sting performed 'Message in a Bottle' and 'Roxanne' at The Secret Policeman's Other Ball concerts in 1981 at the Drury Lane Theatre in London.

Sting, who had been an ambassador for Amnesty International since 1981, performed in all six concerts on the 'Conspiracy of Hope' tour – the first three with his own band and the last three with The Police, who re-formed especially for the performances – culminating with a concert at Giants Stadium in New Jersey on 15 June 1986. Opening with 'Message in a Bottle', the first thing one notices within the first few seconds of the Giants Stadium performance is the negative body language of the band. Unlike earlier performances during their prime, there are few smiles and minimal eye contact, the feel of the whole event being of Sting working with a backing band – each performer in his own private space. Although very much in the background on the TV footage, a number of additional performers, who were introduced by Sting alongside Andy Summers (presented first) and Stewart Copeland (presented last), were included in the performance. 'Message in a Bottle' was followed by 'King of Pain', 'Driven to Tears', 'Every Breath You Take', 'Roxanne' and then 'Invisible Sun'. This set, however, has to be considered very much pure entertainment, rather than political, the band visibly performing for the greater cause – that is, raising finance and increasing awareness. As the conflicts of the members of The Police are well documented, in particular between Sting and Copeland, they will not be covered here, but it would have been no surprise to anyone watching that this would be the last official concert they would undertake until their reunion tour in 2007.[6]

Immediately after The Police had finished their set, Bono introduced eighteen prisoners of conscience, who had been released thanks to the work of Amnesty International; he welcomed them to the stage alongside the star performers involved in the concert. Playing Bob Dylan's 'I Shall Be Released', with the ex-prisoners holding hands, Sting sings the second verse, standing alongside Bryan Adams. The alternating vocals between the numerous star performers are reminiscent of the Live Aid event, which was held the previous year. By this point in the evening's performance, Sting was at the front of the stage alongside the likes of Bono, Peter Gabriel, Joni Mitchell, Joan Baez and Yoko

Sting performing at the Conspiracy of Hope Concert at Giants Stadium, 1986.

Ono – a gesture which symbolically represented how he had eclipsed his fellow Police members in star quality by this point. As we will see, Sting was to distance himself partially from this type of interaction in future Amnesty International concerts. Rather than highlighting only star presence and entertainment, he would compose music that attempted to resonate directly with the audiences he was addressing.

A review of the six concerts, which were dedicated to six specific prisoners of conscience, complies with this mindset, highlighting the seeming importance of entertainment value to the audiences and the lack of original political material. The reviewer described the first concert at the Cow Palace in San

Francisco as featuring 'more than five hours of luminescent, socially aware rock and roll', with 'No new anthems being written to celebrate the cause'.[7] He continued 'none is needed. These are performers who have already spoken through their music.'[8] Although many of the performers had written political content in the past, 'I Shall Be Released' was the key song reappropriated for this new context, closing the last of the six concerts at Giants Stadium. Despite the commendable intentions of the tour, the reviewer highlighted arguably the main dichotomy inherent in concerts of this nature. Although not directed at Sting, the statement typifies the issue:

> To suggest that anyone is here to further their own careers would be the worst form of cynicism. But by the time this tour is over, Gabriel should be a major star – these performances will expose him to the masses he has yet failed to reach, and his musical loquaciousness and fiery performance will gain him scores of new fans. While many people will leave these shows with the urge to send $25 to Amnesty, suspicions are that far more will first choose to spend their money on Gabriel's phenomenal new album.[9]

When Sting was questioned about the tour, he shed some light on this, stating that 'without freedom of expression we [the musicians] can't do our jobs . . . It's [the concerts] for us as well as the people who are being tortured.'[10] Describing Amnesty International as 'probably the most civilized organization in the history of the world', he continued to highlight the importance of ensuring future concerts were unique – possibly hinting at the value of original composition:

> There's no sense in repeating things year after year. If we had done Live Aid again this year we would have gotten

diminishing returns. If musicians and artists are going to be involved in human rights and causes, then each time we do it we have to be creative, innovative, because people get bored. It's our responsibility to make them interested, constantly excited by what's happening.[11]

This not only arguably marks the transition of Sting writing more specific musical content for the causes that interested him, but depicts another tension that was highlighted earlier – the free thinking of the masses. When one reporter asserted 'that this need for perpetual entertainment doesn't say a whole lot for the audience's intelligence or commitment', Sting replied 'No . . . it doesn't.'[12]

Sting also participated in the Human Rights Now! concerts two years later, which took place over a six-week period between 2 September and 15 October 1988; he travelled the world alongside Bruce Springsteen, Peter Gabriel, Youssou N'Dour and Tracy Chapman, once again on behalf of Amnesty International. As with the previous tour, the mission concerned raising awareness of the continuing abuse of human rights by some governments, although this time it did not focus on fundraising. The reason for this was that, unlike the previous tour, many of the concerts also took place in oppressed or developing countries, including India, Zimbabwe and Argentina, all ticket prices being subsidized. In order to make up what would have been a financial deficit, The Reebok Human Rights Foundation acted as tour sponsors.[13] During their visit, which marked the fortieth anniversary of the Universal Declaration of Human Rights, Sting and his fellow stars were introduced to former political prisoners and what he described as 'victims of torture and imprisonment without trial'.[14] He commented, 'It's one thing to read about torture but quite another to speak to a victim and be brought a step closer to a reality that is so frighteningly pervasive. We were deeply affected.'[15]

Examination of concert footage from the final concert of the tour, at River Plate Stadium in Buenos Aires, reveals Sting performing an extended version of 'Don't Stand So Close to Me', closely followed by 'They Dance Alone (*Cueca* Solo)' – the latter, an original composition, was sung and introduced in Spanish. Originally recorded on . . . *Nothing Like the Sun*, the song was inspired by the women who perform the traditional Chilean courting dance (the *Cueca*) alone, with pictures of their dead husbands, fathers and sons pinned to their chests.[16] Although originally released in English, with a single section spoken in Spanish, it was later released in Spanish as part of the EP . . . *Nada como el sol* (1988), entitled 'Ellas danzan solas (cueca sola)'. Unlike the comment made from the journalist earlier regarding the lack of songs specifically written for the new context, 'They Dance Alone (*Cueca* Solo)' is an overt protest against Augusto Pinochet (1915 2006), and was also played live at the Embrace of Hope concert at the National Stadium, Santiago, Chile in 1990.

Although it was not possible to visit Chile in 1988, the Embrace of Hope concert celebrated the end of the Pinochet dictatorship, taking place only seven months after Pinochet handed over the presidency, in March 1990. As with the previous concert, numerous Chilean women appeared on stage with Sting and Peter Gabriel, who danced with the women in turn to an uptempo Latin rhythm. Despite its emotional beginning, the symbolic message at this point in both arrangements is unquestionably optimistic: the women are no longer dancing alone. The two performances have some key differences, however: aside from the earlier concert featuring Sting playing guitar and generally looking more 'groomed', the second performance appears far less staged, essentially appearing more authentic. This may be due partially to the National Stadium being the very location 'where so many had been imprisoned, tortured and killed', one of the 'few venues in the world that is still used though it was a

prison of brutality'.[17] By 1990 this song had become closely associated with the plight of the Chilean nation, not only because of
public performances, but because of the song's associated video,
which would have received heavy rotation on MTV, and the popularity of . . . *Nothing Like the Sun*, which achieved top-ten status
in many territories throughout the world. During the second
performance in Santiago, both Peter Gabriel and Sting appear
emotionally drained by the significance of the concert taking
place in front of the Chilean people in this infamous venue.
Whereas Sting's star presence arguably dominated the politics in
the first, this was not the case in the second.

The location of the concert in Buenos Aires on 15 October
1988 is also significant, as it is in a country to which many Chileans
fled during the Pinochet regime. It features a duet with Sting's
friend Bruce Springsteen on 'Every Breath You Take'. Despite its
well-known theme of surveillance, the song is delivered in a very

Sting performing 'They Dance Alone' as part of the 1988 Human Rights Now! concert.

celebratory mode. In this context, the arrangement almost suggests that it is the oppressed people who are now watching their oppressors! This has a resonance with Sting's earlier arrangement of the song for the UK satirical TV series *Spitting Image*. Entitled 'Every Bomb You Make', and acting as the closing sequence of the end of the final show of the first season of the series (broadcast on 17 June 1984), the arrangement represents an overt attempt by both the TV programme and Sting to subvert the widely popular song towards a political narrative. Sting gave permission not only to use the song, but to re-record it with new lyrics. Beginning with the opening line of 'Every Bomb You Make, Every Job You Take', the arrangement progresses to include phrases such as 'Every War You Build', 'Every Heart You Break', 'Every Irish Wake', 'Everyone You've Killed' and 'Every Grave You've Filled' – all of which end with the famous line taken from the original song – 'I'll Be Watching You'. Although it is initially unclear who the 'I' is, the chorus provides a further clue,

Sting performing 'They Dance Alone' as part of the An Embrace of Hope Concert in 1990.

stating that the perpetrators 'belong to me' and that there will be a bill to pay on judgement day. Considering Sting's Catholic upbringing, it would be logical to think of the protagonist of the song as being a judgemental God, who will make humanity pay for their evil deeds. However, the images of the closing sequence of the *Spitting Image* episode provide an interesting twist. After showing a montage of the black-and-white caricatures of world leaders over the background of a colourful sunset, the final image is that of the Grim Reaper, who appears to the words 'I'll Be Watching You', just prior to the credits. The images of this sequence are obviously not random, but carefully synced to the music, with Ronald Reagan linked to bombs, Margaret Thatcher to jobs, Arthur Scargill and Ian MacGregor to 'broken hearts', Ian Paisley to 'Irish Wakes', Leonid Brezhnev to metaphorical walls, Robert Mugabe to killing, Fidel Castro to the 'filling of graves' and Colonel Gaddafi to the spilling of blood. Commencing with the familiar opening phrase of 'Oh Can't You See', the chorus of the song begins with an image of Yuri Andropov, president of the Soviet Union between 1982 and his death in 1984, followed by Idi Amin (to the words 'You Belong to Me'), culminating in an image of an elderly Adolf Hitler, poignantly linked to the words 'on that judgement day'. The remainder of the song progresses to link Indira Gandhi to empty plates, Ayatollah Khomeini to hateful words and P. W. Botha to those who subjugate, before finishing on the then-current president of the Soviet Union, Konstantin Chernenko – once again to the words 'I'll Be Watching You'. Unlike the majority of content on *Spitting Image*, which was satirical to the point of being frivolously cruel, this was unquestionably a well-thought-out, serious gesture, which in many ways pointed back to the political engagement Sting had already started with The Secret Policeman's Other Ball and 'Murder by Numbers', in addition to being a forerunner to the political content on *The Dream of the Blue Turtles* and his political activism via live performance.

On 16 January 2001 the *Daily Mirror* reported on Sting being 'honoured by Chile for his human rights protests during General Augusto Pinochet's dictatorship'.[18] Mentioning the song 'They Dance Alone', the article includes a statement from then-Foreign Minister Soledad Alvear: 'Sting made an important contribution to informing the world about our country's situation in prior decades.'[19] In recognition of his achievements, Sting is reported to have received the Gabriela Mistral Medal, a human rights award named after the Chilean poet and winner of the Nobel Prize in literature in 1945.

Commenting on Sting's service to Amnesty International and human rights in general, Jack Healey regarded Sting along with Peter Gabriel as his 'anchors in music while [he was] Director of Amnesty International USA'.[20] He also outlines how Sting 'studied Amnesty International literature', 'They Dance Alone' being one of the responses to his knowledge and awareness. Discussing the history behind the song and its impact, Healey stated,

> Mothers of the Plaza de Mayo, who for 16 straight years held weekly demonstrations in front of the Government House to keep alive the memory of their husbands and sons who had . . . disappeared. The song became an international anthem against Pinochet, the dictator of Chile. Much like the song 'Biko' by Peter Gabriel came to be the international voice against apartheid, 'They Dance Alone' went up and down the Americas in much the same way.[21]

During the Human Rights Now! tour, Healey also discussed how the penultimate performance, in Mendoza, Argentina, was, in fact, a tactical location because of its close proximity to the Chilean border:

as our Human Rights Now tour buses left the airport, the
road was lined by the Mothers of the Plaza of Argentina and
Chile. We played in the town of Mendoza so that folks could
come over from Chile. Pinochet would not let us into Chile,
so this was our answer to him. More than 60,000 came to that
concert.[22]

In more recent times, Sting was one of a host of celebrities to
sign an Amnesty International call to release Pussy Riot members Nadezhda Tolokonnikova and Maria Alyokhina, who were
imprisoned for holding a protest concert in a Moscow church in
2012. Two years later, in 2014, alongside Peter Gabriel, Sting was
involved in a pre-taped message for a New York-based Amnesty
International event entitled 'Bringing Human Rights Home'.
Sting and Gabriel were positioned in the event alongside fellow
long-time human rights activists Yoko Ono, Blondie, Bob Geldof
and Susan Sarandon, in a gesture of 'passing the torch' to a
new generation of artists such as Imagine Dragons and Cold
War Kids, with The Flaming Lips closing the event. Although
not directly involved, Sting confirmed his commitment to the
organization:

> More than 30 years ago, we loosened apartheid's grip
> by taking to the stage for the first round of Amnesty
> International human rights concerts. There's still a lot of
> work to be done and Amnesty International is the right place
> to start.[23]

Although Sting's time with The Police was his most commercially successful, in terms of both duration and breadth of
creative output, his solo career represents by far his most varied
and substantive body of work. Officially commencing in 1985, as
of 2017 Sting has passed his thirtieth year as a solo artist, during

which he has produced twelve studio albums, not to mention a significant number of compilation recordings, live albums, movie soundtracks and guest appearances. Examined retrospectively, Sting's solo career has to be considered as a concerted attempt to position himself more clearly as a serious artist, focusing on a far broader range of subjects and musical styles than was possible with The Police.

Sting can be seen to be engaging with an overt political narrative immediately, with *The Dream of the Blue Turtles*, released just over a year after the *Spitting Image* montage and featuring three songs that are worthy of our attention: 'Russians', 'Children's Crusade' and 'We Work the Black Seam'. The subjects of these three songs are an interesting combination, focusing on both local and more global concerns.

As stated earlier, Sting recorded 'We Work the Black Seam' around the time of the miners' strike of 1984–5, and he firmly positions himself as 'one of the community of miners' in the song's narrative, with repeated use of pronouns such as 'us', 'we' and 'our', while clearly placing the Conservative government in opposition, with words such as 'they', 'your' and 'you'. Throughout the song, Sting alludes to how the miners' 'blood has stained the coal', how the government's 'economic theory makes no sense' and how in a future nuclear age the government will understand the miners' rage. He continues to allude to how the closure of the coal mines effectively 'made redundant' the miners' skills, in addition to poisoning the 'streams in Cumberland'. In an interview shortly after the strike reached its resolution, Sting continued with this 'us/them' narrative, clearly outlining the relationship of the song's lyric to his background in Newcastle.

The area I was brought up in was literally built on coal. There are 300 years of coal supplies left, and they're closing all these pits. And five miles from where I lived they're now building a nuclear power station, where they have to import uranium from South Africa. And I frankly think the government has got its head up its arse. They're destroying communities that are culturally very rich. And the government's offering them no alternative, saying you're completely useless.[24]

Regarding the emergence of nuclear technology, he continued,

Those [nuclear] machines were turned on 20 years ago and they don't know how to turn them off. Now they're falling to bits and they don't know how to repair them. It's frightening. There are too many stories of kids with leukaemia around power stations for it to be just rumour, just superstition. The good thing is that people are catching on. I was actually pro nuclear power at one time. I thought, well, it's clean, it's efficient. Until you actually start investigating it, it just takes a little bit of nous to realise we're having the wool pulled over our eyes.[25]

In congruence with the 'us and them' narrative, a small section of the lyrics of 'We Work the Black Seam' are clearly influenced by William Blake's poem 'And Did Those Feet in Ancient Time' (1804), which juxtaposes the concept of a 'New Jerusalem' against those 'dark satanic mills' – essentially the beauty of heaven against the establishment and the Albion Flour Mills, one of the first factories in London.[26] Sting's incorporation of the phrase 'your dark Satanic Mills' in verse two is obviously derived from Blake, only extending Blake's original meaning to that of the impact of nuclear technologies on both the work force and the coal-mining tradition. Discussing the meaning of the poem, an article in *The Guardian* in 2012 outlined how the Albion Flour Mills had local relevance to Blake: 'every time he walked into the City of London he would have passed by the blackened and roofless shell of the Albion Flour Mills that stood for 18 years after being burned down in 1791'.[27] The article then continues to describe how the Industrial Revolution affected the traditional mill workers and the local community's response to industrialization.

> The mill, only five years old when it burned down and equipped with the latest steam-powered rotary machinery, could grind wheat night and day . . . Arson was suspected: it was said local millers were seen dancing on Blackfriars bridge in the light of the flames.[28]

The description has a noticeable resemblance to some mining communities' response to the death of Margaret Thatcher, seen by many as responsible for the closure of many coal mines. For example, the Durham miners' website reported on a party held by Easington Colliery, a mine which eventually closed in 1993, having a devastating impact on the local economy:

> Lighting fags and calling out throaty greetings, men assembled in black t-shirts emblazoned with pictures of gravestones, with slogans saying 'A generation of trade unionists will dance on Thatcher's grave'. There will be no tears or tributes for the Iron Lady here.[29]

These comments, of course, resonate not only with Sting's comments above, but with the ideology underlining 'We Work the Black Seam'.

Sting would likely have studied the Blake poem at grammar school, and appears to have made a clear connection between 'And Did Those Feet in Ancient Time' and the impact of government policy and technological development on contemporary local communities. In addition to the use of 'dark satanic mills', he also alludes more subtly to other parts of the poem with phrases such as 'We walk through ancient forest lands' (verse two) and 'the turning world will sing their souls to sleep' (verse four), which are similar to 'and did those feet in ancient time' and 'nor shall my sword sleep in my hand'. Aside from the lyrical content, Sting also incorporates techniques in order to ensure that the musical background accentuates the subject. For example, the opening repeated keyboard/percussion figure that continues throughout the song appears to be deliberately industrial, with a mechanized avoidance of feeling. This is intersected by the incorporation of a brass band in the choruses – an ensemble closely associated by tradition with many coal mines in England and Wales and previously used by artists such as Peter Skellern and Brian and Michael to depict images of 'northern-ness'.[30] With the release of *Symphonicities* in 2010, Sting incorporated this device more profoundly in an extended brass band arrangement of the song, accompanied only by percussion.

Although the verses of the song are clearly addressing the Conservative government, the chorus, through lines such as 'One day in a nuclear age, they may understand our rage', appears to be directed towards the miners, accentuating the positioning of the protagonist of the song as 'one of the people', as opposed to one of 'them'. Finally, although Sting delivers the song in an accent that is generally difficult to place in terms of location, his use of the word 'suck' in the final verse is deliberately delivered in a northeastern accent. This not only alludes to the fact that the song is targeted towards the northeast of England, but it makes the word stand out – although what he means by 'the universe will suck me into place' is debatable. Interestingly, this song has been re-arranged by a number of folk artists such as Kevin Burke and Ged Foley (*In Tandem*, 2005), The Battlefield Band (*Celtic Hotel*, 1987) and Pat Kilbride (*Rock and More Roses*, 1990). This indicates not only that the song is imbued with authenticity, but that it has a universal theme, the subject having strong resonances with North American-based songs such as '16 Tons' and 'Dark as a Dungeon' by Merle Travis, as well as 'A New South Wales' by The Alarm, which also provides a personal account of the negative impact of Thatcherism, only this time related to the mining communities of South Wales.

The song 'Russians' includes clear references to Cold War history, with the line 'Mr Khrushchev said we will bury you' representing a paraphrase of a speech Khrushchev gave in November 1956 while addressing Western ambassadors in Moscow.[31] Sting's problematic position and knowledge of American politics at the time are also alluded to in lines such as 'there is no historical precedent, to put words in the mouth of the president'. During the mid-1980s, this was something that was regularly targeted on *Spitting Image*, which depicted President Reagan as an absent-minded old man who did not have a mind of his own. Controversially, in his memoirs of 2008, Press Secretary Larry Speaks, who was involved in the historic meetings between Reagan and Mikhail Gorbachev, asserted that he had put words into the president's mouth by 'polishing the quotes'.[32] Sting then includes the phrase 'there is no such thing as a winnable war' – clearly using Reagan's famous phrase, while contesting the president's belief that a nuclear war with the Soviet Union was 'winnable': 'Mister Reagan says we will protect you, I don't subscribe to this point of view.' Discussing the song, Sting outlined to *The Independent* that some of its background was related to a time when he was living in New York:

> a friend of mine had a gizmo that could pull the signal from the Russian satellite. We'd go drinking and then watch Russian morning shows in the middle of the night. It was apparent from watching these lovingly made kids' shows that Russians weren't quite the automatons that we'd been told they were.[33]

Sting described the song at the time as not pro-American or pro-Russian, but pro-children, a statement which is encapsulated in the phrase 'How can I save my little boy from Oppenheimer's deadly toy' – clearly a reference to his son Joseph and by extension all his listeners' children. Additionally, although the song has no chorus, the refrain of the verses ends with the plea that Sting 'hope[s] that the Russians love their children too' – as that is the only factor that will save the world from destruction. In congruence with Sting's position as a 'world citizen', 'Russians' is a first-person narrative plea to both sides ('There is no monopoly in common sense, on either side of the political fence'), the central theme being not only the futility of war, but the suspect propaganda surrounding the West's depiction of the Russian nation. Interviewed in 2011 on Russian TV, Sting commented,

> I was born and brought up in the west, and we were educated and conditioned to look at the Soviet Union as an ideological fortress . . . and also because they were ideological enemies . . . it's easier to fight a war against people who perhaps aren't quite human . . . I was aware that that was happening to me, in the media – in education generally.[34]

On a more musical level, after the sampled narrative of state broadcaster Igor Kirillov at the start of the song (juxtaposed against a ticking clock), 'Russians' also subtly incorporates the 'Romance' theme from Prokofiev's *Lieutenant Kijé* after each refrain of 'I hope the Russians love their Children too'. In addition to simply 'sounding Russian', Sting is expecting a certain type of cultural literacy from his listeners when quoting a theme such as this from high culture – a factor he would arguably have been eager to foster at the start of his solo career, although its inclusion could be regarded as an act of protest in itself.[35] Interestingly, themes from *Lieutenant Kijé* have also been used by artists such

as Greg Lake, who used the melody from the Troika theme in
'I Believe in Father Christmas' (1974) and Blood, Sweat & Tears,
whose '40,000 Headmen' (1970) incorporates the melody from the
second movement 'Romance'. As with 'We Work the Black Seam',
Sting is displaying his literacy with this gesture, although quoting
music out of context was arguably something he was experiment-
ing with at the time, with 'Love Is the Seventh Wave' referencing
his own 'Every Breath You Take'.[36]

During the mid-1980s, Sting was not the only famous musician
commenting on President Reagan's politics. In his autobiography,
Frank Zappa also regularly and strongly passes judgement upon
incompetent governments, which captures the zeitgeist perfectly.[37]
Other musical examples include Zappa's own 'Reagan at Bitburg',
in addition to songs such as The Ramones' 'My Brain is Hanging
Upside Down (Bonzo Goes to Bitburg)', Bruce Springsteen's 'Born
in the USA' and Prince's 'Ronnie, Talk to Russia'.[38]

The first few minutes of 'Children's Crusade' appears on the
surface to extend the futility of war theme of 'Russians' – with
the constant reiteration of the word 'poppies' initially seeming
to allude to the graves of dead soldiers who lost their lives during
the First World War. As outlined by Christopher Gable, the poppy
was famously used as a symbol of war by John McRae in his poem
'Flanders Fields' (1915), although there is no evidence that this was
a direct influence on Sting.[39] It is only during the song's last verse
that one realizes that the poppy is being incorporated additionally
as an allusion to the Soho-based opium addiction problem which
was emerging in London at the time: 'Midnight in Soho . . . fixing
in doorways, opium slaves . . . all of those young lives betrayed.'
In light of this final verse, the song can also be considered a
powerful and shocking anti-drug statement, in the tradition of
pieces such as The Velvet Underground's 'Heroin' (1967), Neil
Young's 'The Needle and the Damage Done' (1972) and the Red
Hot Chili Peppers' 'Knock Me Down' (1989). Commenting on

the song, Sting confirmed this anti-war/drug rhetoric, but also revealed a third strand to his political narrative:

> I tried to combine an . . . interest in the First World War, heroin addiction in contemporary London, and the abuse of twelfth-century street children, who were sold into slavery in a cynical pseudo religious scam that is appalling even by the low moral standards of the Crusaders and the ethics of the time. There seemed to be a connection.[40]

Sting is describing what some consider the legendary attempt of young Christians from France and Germany travelling to the Holy Land to expel Muslims or convert them to Christianity. The children believed they were protected by God – who would, by a series of miracles, give them the power to travel to Jerusalem and fulfil their objective. Occurring in 1212, the Crusade was not successful – many of the children died from exhaustion or were sold into slavery. The authenticity of the medieval story Sting is describing in 'Children's Crusade' is not important, but can be considered part of a broader anti-religion theme, which is possibly fuelled by the negative experiences he went through in school.[41]

Although the first two verses of 'Children's Crusade' appear to be overtly aligned to the First World War, with Sting commenting on how the war resulted in inexperienced young men marching through countries 'they had never seen', it is now easy to make the connection with the Crusade of 1212 and its broader anti-religion context. These young men are described as 'pawns in the game' controlled by 'corpulent generals [who are] safe behind lines'. Considering Sting's problematic relationship with Christianity, it is easy to consider the 'game' as religion, and the 'corpulent generals' as church leaders. This relationship is confirmed by his repeated use of 'all for a children's crusade' in both verses – which now makes perfect sense from the tripartite perspective intended by Sting.

The Dream of the Blue Turtles was followed by . . . *Nothing Like the Sun* (1987), written shortly after Sting's involvement in Amnesty International's 'Conspiracy of Hope' tour. In addition to 'They Dance Alone', this album features 'History Will Teach Us Nothing' and 'Fragile', both songs that have a strong political narrative and, interestingly, are placed next to each other in the album running order. 'History Will Teach Us Nothing' portrays a cynical view of history by highlighting the tendency of the human race to pursue comfort in 'human systems' and, most importantly, of not learning from the mistakes of tyrannical leaders. Performed in a reggae style obviously influenced by Bob Marley, the subject highlights the importance of reason over 'blind faith' and political power – the headline of the song asserts that otherwise 'history will teach us nothing'. The song concludes with the phrase 'know your human rights, be what you come here for', which when performed live on the tour promoting . . . *Nothing Like the Sun*, segued into Bob Marley's 'Get Up Stand Up' at the end, a song which would become the show opener at the Human Rights Now! concerts in 1988. Although originally written in response to a newspaper report regarding the death of an American engineer working in Nicaragua who was murdered by the Contras, 'Fragile' is a song that has transcended its original inspiration, being adopted by the ecology movement and more poignantly in the wake of the Twin Towers 9/11 terrorist attacks. The latter reappropriation of the song was captured on Sting's *All This Time* DVD, recorded live from his Tuscan home in a week-long rehearsal at the end of *Brand New Day* tour.[42] Although the intention of the rehearsals was to have a live webcast celebrating reworked renditions of his music, the World Trade Center attacks resulted in 'Fragile' being the only song that was broadcast, as a mark of respect for the victims. Examining the lyrical content, the unintentional resonance with the Twin Towers attacks is palpable, with lines such as 'tomorrow's rain will wash the stains away', 'nothing comes from violence and nothing ever could'; the statement outlining 'how fragile we are' is particularly poignant. Sting, of course, has lived in New York for many years, so these attacks would have been very personal.

Despite its sociopolitical comment, Sting claimed to have written . . . *Nothing Like the Sun* 'for himself alone'. He continued,

> I hope my music is something I would make anyway. If I wasn't successful I hope I would still be writing these songs. I write for myself and if the audience likes it, that's wonderful.[43]

This perspective has been challenged by the cynical national press over the years, who have heavily criticized Sting for his political activism. In 1993, an article in *The Times* reflects on the response of the national press to Sting's political activism in the mid-1980s:

> Sting's announcement that he was setting up a foundation to raise public awareness of the devastation of Brazil's rain forests, in particular the Xingu Park, an area of native land the size of Switzerland, gave them [the press] the impetus to wound. He was a do-gooder, a dilettante; worst of all, a bore . . . 'What a career move,' cynics hissed, as he introduced heads of state and chat-show hosts to Chief Raoni, leader of the Kayapo tribe, whom they would remember more for the plate that distended his bottom lip than for the dignity of his pleas for the protection of his people and their environment.[44]

The article continues to describe Sting's work with the Rainforest Foundation as being perceived as 'a self-aggrandising global photo-opportunity':

the one-time rock hero was now Eco-Sting, a cartoon-like caped crusader flying around in loincloth and body paint, hellbent on saving the planet from destruction. We British, preferring our environmentalists to look like Attenborough or Bellamy, chortled with ill-concealed delight.[45]

The article then attempts to summarize the 'issues' associated with Sting:

Few of us take kindly to being reminded of our inadequacies and ill-formed attitudes. We enjoy the process still less when the hectoring voice belongs to someone who, although a contemporary in age, is far richer, far more celebrated, and infinitely more glamorous than ourselves. That, one supposes, is why so many people in Britain have come to think of Sting as smug, pretentious, a bit of a clever-dick. And, if we examine our consciences, we will admit that there are few things we Britons like less.[46]

The 'issues' outlined above are related to Sting's political activism as opposed to his music, but it seems that the two can be inextricably linked. For example, in a later article in 2000 for the *Sunday Times*, the author traces the protest song as commencing with Bob Dylan's album *Freewheelin'* of 1963, asserting, 'he [Dylan] provided the impetus for everyone with an afghan coat to pick up a guitar and start moaning.'[47] After describing how an unnamed Donovan song had waxed lyrical about the 'American bombing raids over Hanoi' and how Barry McGuire (presumably via his song 'Eve of Destruction') informed him 'that his [the songwriter's] blood was so mad it felt like coagulating', the article then proposes that 'the protest song seems to have gone away.'[48] Although letting rap music and Bruce Springsteen off the hook, the author gets around to criticizing environmentalism, leading eventually to Sting:

The trouble is, though, since Sting decided to promote his new CD by sewing it into the bottom lip of an Amazonian tribesman, singing about trees has been seen as a bit uncool.[49]

Reviewing *Sacred Love* in 2003, a *Daily Mirror* article takes a long time to get around to discussing his music, which was actually very positive, opening up with the description of a 'condition' that 'every music lover at one time or another' has experienced, describing it as 'SAS (Sting Allergic Syndrome)', with 'symptoms' including 'involuntary shudders of jealousy and/or revulsion towards the man formerly known as Gordon Sumner'.[50] The reasons for this troubled relationship with the general public are seen to range from pomposity, to filming the birth of his children, to attempting to copyright his stage name and his charity work with the Rainforest Foundation and Amnesty International, the latter of which was 'seen as evidence of a holier than thou stance'.[51] Five years later, in a readers' poll in *The Independent* in 2008, Sting's humanitarian mission was still receiving bad press – this time via the general public, with only one-third of readers considering he had made a 'worthwhile contribution to green causes' and with the majority thinking he made 'no difference'.[52] The same year, *The Guardian*, while noting the landmark twentieth anniversary of Sting's Rainforest Foundation, proceeds to report on the 'criticism over the way the charity network is being managed':

> The watchdog's main criticism was that in 2006 the US foundation spent only 60% of its funds on actual programmes on the ground – compared with a sector norm of 75%. A watchdog spokeswoman said its records showed that the foundation did even worse in 2004 when 43% of its revenues were spent on such projects.[53]

An edition of *Newsnight* originally shown on the BBC on 1 December 2009 and covering Sting's 'return' to the rainforest typifies this position. Instead of focusing on the positives, the programme intersects coverage of his rainforest visit with charges of hypocrisy, this time particularly focusing on his carbon footprint, mentioning 'claims' that The Police (who had recently completed their reunion tour) were 'the most polluting band on earth'.[54] Asked if he felt uncomfortable about his carbon footprint, Sting commented,

> I think it is an amusing red herring for the media to blame celebrities for the global crisis we are in. I have done a lot of work to safeguard vast amounts of Equatorial rainforests over the past 20 years. I think I have tried to ameliorate my carbon footprint, which is admittedly large.[55]

In 2012 Sting was also branded a hypocrite by the *Daily Mail*, because of images, taken in Damascus in 2008, that pictured him 'laughing and joking with brutal Syrian dictator President Al-Assad'.[56] Although Sting is quoted as stating he was '"disgusted" by the brutality of his military regime', the article concludes by mentioning a concert in Uzbekistan in 2010, which was organized by the regime of Islam Karimov (then president of the country and widely criticized for his human rights record), in which he was reportedly paid £2 million.[57]

These accusations bring to the surface the whole issue of whether rock stars should get involved in politics: it was a classic case of 'damned if you do and damned if you don't'. Similarly, Sting's close friend Paul Simon received critical and commercial success with his album *Graceland* of 1986. Its sophisticated musicianship, postmodern combination of styles, use of jazz musicians and intercultural cooperation introduced many listeners to the sounds of South Africa for the first time, with Simon even passing

on 'revenues from the album's promotional tour to support char-
itable projects in Africa and in African-American communities'.[58]
Despite these honourable intentions, Simon, and by default the
album, also received criticism for complying with hegemonic
Western power relations. Concisely speaking, Simon and his
Western-based music industry representatives were deemed still
to have the controlling power in terms of who had access to
resources such as marketing, finance, technology and intellectual
property ownership.

Alongside the countless other artists who have incorporated
influences from non-European countries into their music, Sting
could be seen to be taking indigenous musical influences and
reappropriating them for his own artistic ends. Alongside the likes
of Bono and Peter Gabriel, he can also be judged to be exploiting
political situations in countries such as Chile and using them to
publicize his career. However, political song (in both live and
recorded format) and activism can also be considered a symbolic
act of solidarity with the countries or localities represented. The
dilemma of the positive or negative impact of these practices to
a large extent depends on the perception of the 'critic', but what
is apparent is that Sting only became involved in activism when
he was already an established artist. For this writer, the issue is
more a reflection of the Western capitalist societies that have
emerged over the last hundred years or so, of which the music
industries are a part. Artists such as Sting simply operate within
this globalized context. How is it possible to tour the world promoting your music and not have a carbon footprint? Why should
artists not draw upon a wide range of global influences in their
music? Indeed, has this not always been the case in popular music,
with its foundational bedrock, the blues, representing a fusion of
African and European influences? The reasons for Sting's press
and media criticisms are complex, ranging from the inability
of the UK press and media to understand or appreciate political

altruism, to simple jealousy, to the distrust of multimillionaire musicians and to the inability of audiences and media outlets to understand the subaltern populations that are outside of the dominant power structures of the West. I would say that although it would be naive to suggest that there was no publicity imperative in some of Sting's early charity work from a management perspective, activities such as his incorporation of Chilean women dancing the *cueca* or of raï influences on 'Desert Rose' does not decontextualize the music and traditions of oppressed countries or indeed exploit them, but rather continues the homogenization process that has been so pervasive since popular music started.

The homogenization of different musical styles, so noticeable in Sting's solo career in particular, was obviously fuelled by the various parts of the world he frequented. So it is interesting to note that despite these numerous experiences and influences, it is his roots in Newcastle that have dominated his recent creative impulses. This will be the focus of the final chapter.

Publicity photo of The Police inside NYPD 28th police precinct in 1979.

CONCLUSION:
FROM AMERICA TO THE MAGNETIC NORTH

In 1979 The Police were making a concerted attempt to break America, touring the country three times and spending 135 days there in total that year. The year 1979 also saw them become more established in London, performing at larger venues such as the Hammersmith Odeon and headlining the Reading Festival on 24 August 1979. That same month saw the re-release of 'Can't Stand Losing You' reaching number two in the UK charts, building on the number twelve success of 'Roxanne' in May. This success was partially fuelled by Sting's increasing public presence outside music – the film *Quadrophenia* was released shortly after their Reading performance on 14 September. That month The Police would experience their first UK number 1 with 'Message in a Bottle'. With a video that was shot at Kennedy Space Center on 23 October during their third American tour, 'Walking on the Moon' was to become the second UK number one for The Police in December 1979, although the record failed to chart in the United States.

The Police's first 'top ten' single successes in the US were to be the following year, with 'Don't Stand So Close to Me' and 'De Do Do Do, De Da Da Da', both of which reached number ten in the Billboard Top 100 towards the end of 1980. 'Every Little Thing She Does Is Magic' was to give The Police their fourth UK number one in October 1981, closely followed by a number three position in America. By the end of the decade, Sting had made his presence in America more permanent, acquiring his first American apartment, an eighteen-room duplex at 88 Central Park West, purchased from Billy Joel for $4.8 million. Interestingly, it was during the late 1980s, a time not only of great financial success, but of acclaim in his solo career, that Sting suffered from his first significant instance of writer's block. It was at this point that he would draw on the places, people and events of his background in Newcastle to light a torch to his creative impulses.

The first Sting-penned song to reach number one on both sides of the Atlantic was 'Every Breath You Take' in 1983, taken from The Police's final and most commercially successful album *Synchronicity*. Sting 'make(s) no claims for any originality' in the song, declaring that 'it shares a chord sequence with a million other songs'.[1] He continued, '[I]'d like to think that power lies in its ambiguity, in it being both seductive and sinister.' He also revealed how his 'life had invaded the song' during its construction.

> Everything around me seemed to be disintegrating: my marriage, my band, my sanity, and this at a time when, from the outside, I appeared to be one of the most successful musicians in the world.[2]

It is well documented that artistic success and substantial financial returns created a number of personal problems for Sting; these eventually resulted in divorce from Frances Tomelty in 1984, in addition to the break-up of The Police. Listening to 'Every Breath You Take', it is indeed noticeably formulaic in structure, having an 'AABA' 'Popular Song Form', which was so pervasive during the Tin Pan Alley period. Comparing it to other songs, arguably the most similar is 'Every Breath I Take' by Gene Pitney. Released in 1961 when Sting was ten, it has a similar turnaround chord progression and lyrical catch phrase, which bear an obvious connection to Sting's song. However, the turnaround chord progression is literally used in hundreds of songs, ranging from the verse of 'Unchained Melody', made famous by The Righteous Brothers (but written in 1955), to Leiber and Stoller's 'Stand by Me' (which was a hit in 1960 for Ben E. King), so the progression and the lyrical content of the Pitney song is likely to have been a subliminal influence during Sting's youth.

Reflecting upon his first visit to New York to play two consecutive nights with The Police at CBGBs in October 1978, Sting saw it as 'the beginning of a life-long love affair', regarding it as a city that intoxicated him like no other, 'a city of the unbridled imagination, of giddy, vertiginous dreams, legendary rudeness, and the vertical drama of social mobility.'[3] It is interesting to consider the American public's and music industry's perceptions of The Police in these early years and their coverage of the emergence of Sting as the band's driving force. In an article for *Trouser Press*, commenting on the first gigs at CBGBs, Jim Green refers to Sting as 'The bassist . . . jumping around in a boiler suit and . . . singing in this neat, kinda high-pitched voice'.[4] Green had obviously heard of the band through their debut single 'Roxanne', although it was not released in America until early 1979, reaching number 32 in April that year, a factor that unquestionably fuelled the success of the re-release of the single the following month in the UK.[5]

The article also makes a point of trying to make sense of the unusual background of the band members – mentioning Stewart Copeland's association with Curved Air and Andy Summers's work with Eric Burdon and the Animals, Zoot Money's Big Roll Band and Soft Machine. Sting at this point appears to be regarded solely as the writer of 'Roxanne', having less noteworthy musical heritage than the other two members. The author then asks an understandable question relating to the perceived authenticity of The Police. Considering the band are performing in one of

America's most iconic punk venues, he poses a question that had been pervasive in the UK: 'what [are] these decidedly non-punks . . . doing in a, well, new wave band?'[6] At that point in the history of The Police, Copeland is seen as the band's leader, the article briefly discussing how he met Sting when he was 'play[ing] with his [unnamed] jazz band' and how they had all played in Mike Howlett's Gong reunion concert six months before. The article concludes by mentioning Sting's 'substantial role in the upcoming *Quadrophenia* film', in addition to 'Roxanne' 'creat[ing] a small stir in some markets like Boston'.[7] When asked how their music has the potential to stand out in America, Andy Summers revealed that The Police had developed a clear philosophy, built around the songs of Sting. After stating how American audiences appear to have been 'alienated or bemused by the excesses of British punk', he revealed how Sting's compositions were beginning to find their niche in America:

> maybe some of the earlier punk bands were too radical a departure from anything Americans had been listening to. Our music falls a bit easier on their ears. We're something of a cross-over between hard-core punk and the more standard rock & roll: not as radical as the Sex Pistols, but definitely not Boston or Foreigner either.[8]

Reflecting on how this change in popularity had occurred, an article in the *New York Rocker* considered The Police to be in 'several ways the right band at the right time', benefiting from a new wave association, but 'eminently [more] programmable [in terms of radio]'.[9] Interestingly, as opposed to questioning the authenticity of the band, their music is now perceived as being a 'natural extension of their own personalities . . . having hit on their own reggae/rock fusion casually, through odd licks tossed around at rehearsal, [it] is believable'.[10]

By 1980 The Police had obviously turned the corner in terms of popularity, with Sting describing himself as 'rich' on a few occasions in an article for *Creem*. Considering why his songs had become so popular, he declared,

> The songs come from life experiences everybody's had. My music is my favourite kind of music. As far as the subject matter goes, it's me. I'm not pretending to be a wild woolly playboy, or a rough rebel, or whatever. The songs are very simple songs about things that have happened to me – songs about loneliness, everybody's felt that, so it had wide appeal.[11]

This comment took place just prior to The Police undertaking a year-long world tour, largely at their own expense, not only in more familiar European and North American territories, but in countries such as Japan, Australia, India, Egypt, Greece, Argentina and Brazil. The year 1980 was also the year Sting became a

Sting and The Police performing at the Palladium, New York City, 29 November 1979.

tax exile on the west coast of Ireland, with a newly purchased home in Hampstead in London an indicator of his new-found wealth. The recording of the third album by The Police (*Zenyatta Mondatta*) between 7 July and 7 August 1980 at the Phillips-founded Wisseloord Studios in Hilversum, the Netherlands, as opposed to the UK-based Surrey Sound, was also reflective of the band's need to become more tax efficient. Adhering to this practice, the next two albums, *Ghost in the Machine* and the majority of *Synchronicity*, were recorded at George Martin's Air Studios on Montserrat Island, 'a stunning realisation of Sting's adolescent fantasy of living in the Caribbean' according to Christopher Sandford.[12]

Carrying on the heavy touring schedule of The Police between 1977 and 1984, Sting has continued to travel the world regularly throughout the thirty years of his solo career, his website listing not only the venues he has frequented, but the number of cities and countries he has visited.[13] At the start of his solo career, his profile as a world megastar enabled him to recruit a group of some of the most prestigious young American jazz musicians for his backing band, including Kenny Kirkland, Omar Hakim and Branford Marsalis. Aside from the overt jazz pedigree of the band, which in many ways alludes to Sting's artistic interests performing with Last Exit in Newcastle, this was a racially integrated band, in which Sting appeared to be deliberately challenging rigid North American media protocols. He commented,

> One of the reasons [popular music is] dead is because it's become very reactionary and racist. Where black musicians are not really given the opportunity to be heard on white radio or in white publications, and it's just as bad the other way. This band . . . is an open challenge to that system.[14]

Ironically, while Sting's 'Blue Turtles' band may have challenged this racially segregated system, The Police could

Sting and The Police performing at The Summit, Houston, Texas, on 17 November 1983.

be considered to have benefited from it. The notorious 'record smashing' 'Disco Demolition Night', hosted by DJ Steve Dahl at Comiskey Park in Chicago, took place on 12 July 1979 – just as The Police were breaking America. During the early months of 1979, disco was the dominant popular music force on both sides of the Atlantic, with acts such as Chic, Sister Sledge, The Village People, Gloria Gaynor and their white counterparts The Bee Gees dominating the charts. This commercial success ran in parallel with a stream of negative feelings towards disco in North America, DJ Dahl being one of the protagonists determined to eradicate what his mock organization 'The Insane Coho Lips' described as 'the dreaded musical disease known as DISCO'.[15] Dahl adopted this stance after losing his job hosting a local rock radio show, which was replaced by a 'disco channel'. Indeed, disco was accused not only of replacing Adult Oriented Rock (AOR) stations in America, but of subverting what was considered the more authentic rock genre – Rod Stewart's 'Do Ya Think I'm Sexy?' was arguably the most famous instance of this practice, prompting Dahl to release a skit, entitled 'Do You Think I'm Disco?' (1979).[16] Although this record was satirical in nature, the subtext to Dahl's activities was regarded by John Rockwell of the *New York Times* as racially motivated; through them, the forces of 'white America' attempted to prohibit the emerging gay liberation and black pride movements associated with disco.[17] According to Chris Campion, Sting and The Police 'found themselves inadvertently leading the charge in the reactionary movement building against disco. No less than their own record company considered them the great white hope to stave off the deluge of urban music.'[18] In many respects, the racial integration of the Blue Turtles band could be considered Sting's way of retrospectively addressing these historic idiosyncrasies of American radio programming.

During the lead up to recording . . . *Nothing Like the Sun* in March 1987, both of Sting's parents were reported to be suffering from cancer in a December 1986 edition of Newcastle's *The Journal*, which reported the following day that Sting was coming back to Newcastle for Christmas to visit them.[19] His father is reported to have passed away on 19 November 1987, the day prior to Sting performing at the Maracanã Stadium in Brazil, three days after the start of his . . . *Nothing Like the Sun* tour. He did not attend the funeral.[20] Sting recalled his mother's illness during the writing of . . . *Nothing Like the Sun* and how this 'strongly influenced [his] creative process':

> Not that the record is in the least bit morbid – my mother would not have wanted to be remembered that way. There is a thread of romance, sadness and fun that characterises the record as well as her life.[21]

Like songs such as John Lennon's 'My Mummy's Dead' (*John Lennon/Plastic Ono Band*, 1970), and Bono's 'Tomorrow' (*October*, 1981), which both deal with the loss of mothers, and albums such as *Magic and Loss* (1992) by Lou Reed and more recently Sufjan Stevens's *Carrie & Lowell* (2015), . . . *Nothing Like the Sun* in many ways represents the symbolization, renegotiation and articulation of personal emotions related to grief.[22] However, Sting deals with his subject less directly and more holistically than some of these other instances, tending to allude to his pain through abstract phrases such as 'but the sword that cut him open, was the sword in his mother's hand' or 'birds on the roof of my mother's house, I've no stones to chase them away', and '[these stones will] sit on [his] roof someday.'[23] Sting also deals with the theme of women elsewhere on the album, ranging from isolated and persecuted women in 'They Dance Alone', to the song 'Sister Moon', which quotes from the famous Shakespearean line 'My mistress's eyes are nothing like the sun', from Sonnet 130. After conceding that his mother's illness was having an impact on his creative impulses, in an interview for *Spin* magazine during the making of the album, Sting revealed that an early name considered for the album was *In Praise of Women*, continuing, 'that's what it is about . . . that's the theme.'[24] The interview with Vic Garbarini is interesting, spanning a number of days before and after his mother's death, into the mixing of the album at New York's Power Station. Although Sting struggles to get constructive work done beforehand, after having been informed of her passing, there is a change in his productivity, described by Garbarini:

> Within two weeks the album has pulled out of its nose-dive. The studio is vibrant with energy as lead vocals are laid down and song arrangements finally come into focus.[25]

In August 1987, in between the passing of his two parents, Sting was reported to be back in Newcastle working on the set of *Stormy Monday*, in which he played a Geordie nightclub boss called Finney with gangster connections. Set mainly in the Quayside area of Newcastle, at a fictitious jazz venue called the Key Club, the movie provided Sting with an opportunity not only to spend an extended amount of time in his hometown to visit friends and relatives, but to engage in some broader, more abstract themes that resonate with Newcastle. For example, the Key Club and Sting's role as Finney allude strongly to the Club A'GoGo, where Sting saw Jimi Hendrix in 1967, and its London-born owner Mike Jeffery, the controversial manager of The Animals, who was actually accused of murdering Hendrix by roadie James 'Tappy' Wright.[26] As its predecessor *Get Carter* (1971) does, the film depicts Newcastle as distinct from 'the south', with the local underworld in conflict with outside interests. During the film, Sting speaks with an authentic Geordie accent, and in many ways, the film can be seen as a step towards his work with *The Last Ship* nearly two decades later.

Sting's website outlines little touring activity taking place over the two-year period 1989–91, a time which he used to come to terms with the deaths of his parents and to establish his Rainforest Foundation, travelling the world with Chief Raoni in order to raise awareness of the plight of the Megkronoti tribe of Kayapo Indians, from the Xingu region of the Amazon. Following in the footsteps of others such as the rubber tappers movement, which had been campaigning since 1975 to guarantee land-use rights and to improve the living standards of Amazon forest peoples, Sting used his celebrity to inform the world of the plight of the rainforest, and of how our negligence has potentially catastrophic consequences not only for the Amazon people, but globally.[27] As with his work for Amnesty International, Sting's efforts were

Sting besieged by autograph hunters during the filming of *Stormy Monday*, at the Quayside in Newcastle, 1987.

often met with disdain in the press, who accused him of taking advantage of the purity and innocence of rainforest Indians and of self-promotion.[28] This two-year period was also a time in which Sting suffered from writer's block, which was finally exorcized when he wrote *The Soul Cages*. As the previous album had, *The Soul Cages* acted as a cathartic means for Sting to come to terms with his identity, past and grief. Speaking of how his father's death had 'hit [him] harder than . . . imagined', he declared,

> I felt emotionally and creatively paralysed, isolated and unable to mourn. I just felt numb and empty, as if the joy had been leached out of my life. Eventually I talked myself into going back to work, and this sombre collection of songs was the result. I became obsessed with my hometown and its history, images of boats and the sea, and my childhood in the shadow of the shipyard.[29]

After touring *The Soul Cages* during the early months of 1991 in the United States, Sting commenced his UK tour in Newcastle at the Buddle Arts Centre in Wallsend on 20 April 1991, a venue at which Sting frequently performed during his time as a local musician and which is on the same street he lived on as a boy. This concert, broadcast live locally on Metro FM with selected tracks released on *Sting: Acoustic Live in Newcastle* (1991), also gave Sting the opportunity to perform with his old Last Exit colleagues. Sting had earlier donated a PA system to the venue in January 1986, while touring *Dream of the Blue Turtles*, providing £10,000 to purchase the sound system, which was used to provide rock music workshops and rehearsal space for struggling musicians in the area.[30]

Interestingly, none of Sting's tours between 2005 and his work with *The Last Ship* introduced new songs, focusing instead on showcasing the work of John Dowland (*Songs from the Labyrinth*, between October 2006 and February 2009), the back catalogue of

The Buddle Arts Centre in 2014.

The Police (reunion tour in 2007–8) or symphonic versions of his portfolio (*Symphonicity* tour of 2010–11). Since then, Sting has dedicated the majority of his creative energy towards *The Last Ship*, the album prequel (2013) to the Broadway show being his first recorded new material in nearly a decade. Work on *The Last Ship* initially began in 2009, when Broadway producer Jeffrey Seller met with Sting, who was considering a theatre production based on his *The Soul Cages* album. Having found further inspiration after reading a newspaper report about a Catholic priest who led a group of homeless shipbuilders to build a ship of their own, Sting sent Seller a demo of the song 'Shipyard', after which it was decided to push forward with the project.

In this work, Sting is clearly paying tribute to the local community of his birthplace through an autobiographical lens, the songs speaking both *from* this community and providing a narrative *about* it. Sting, in fact, asked the opinion of a local audience, including the ex-shipbuilding community of Newcastle, when testing out early drafts of *The Last Ship* between 3 and 4 February 2012 at Newcastle's intimate Live Theatre. The show also undertook a similar process in October 2011 in New York, under the direction of Pulitzer-prize-winning dramatist Brian Yorkey, who wrote the book alongside *Skyfall* screenwriter John Logan. With the early showcases taking place between Newcastle and New York, *The Last Ship* can also be regarded musically as an interesting synthesis of northern English folk culture combined with the harmonic propensities of the American songbook, a tendency that is apparent throughout much of the original album, in particular on songs such as 'Dead Man's Boots' and 'So to Speak', both of which feature complex chordal harmony.[31]

Working on *The Last Ship* must have been a nostalgic experience for Sting, who obviously remembers the shipbuilding communities of his hometown with great fondness. Most importantly, following in the wake of classic shows such as *Oklahoma*, *South Pacific* and *Hello Dolly*, Broadway productions arguably have the potential to trigger feelings of nostalgia for audiences, which is possibly one of the reasons the show failed to resonate fully with the American public. The struggling shipbuilding community of a northern English town, combined with northern England accents, unemployment, economic depression and a lack of escapism appeared simply not to attract or sustain Broadway audiences. In addition to this, the show did not include any of Sting's hits and, despite Jimmy Nail's work with Madonna in the film *Evita* (1996), it did not feature any notable star performers. Although some reviews were positive, attendance figures were low, with concerns about the show's closure prompting Sting to step front of stage, replacing Jimmy Nail as Jackie White on 9 December 2014.[32] However, although ticket sales picked up sharply, Sting's appearances were not enough to save it, the final performance taking place on Saturday 24 January 2015, having played 134 shows at the Neil Simon Theatre since its first preview performance on 29 September 2014. Despite reports of the show's losses for its investors and the script being poor, most critics were supportive of Sting's songs, which subsequently earned him a Tony Award.[33]

Three months after the closure of *The Last Ship* on Broadway, Sting performed three concerts in Newcastle, with songs from the show at Gateshead's Sage venue in April 2015. The concerts were very much positioned as a homecoming, with Sting narrating the story and introducing the characters of the script and their associated songs, but also clearly locating himself as one of the Newcastle people. This was achieved by the numerous stories he recounted regarding the inspiration behind the songs and his family's place within the tradition of shipbuilding in particular; Sting also noted that the Sage was a venue 'us Geordies' were proud of. Cunard supported these concerts, in their 175th year of business, a very apt sponsor considering the shipping company's long historic links to the Swan Hunter shipyard, based in Sting's hometown of Wallsend. Throughout these concerts, which featured other Geordie musicians such as The Wilson Family, Kathryn Tickell, The Unthanks and Jimmy Nail alongside more regular session musicians, Sting sang and spoke in a noticeable northern accent, recounting stories such as the Queen Mother's visit to Wallsend in 1961, which he recalled with humour and fondness.

Throughout *The Last Ship*, resonance with Sting's past is obvious, in particular through the relationship between the Gideon Fletcher character and his father, which is clearly an estranged relationship similar to that of Sting and his own father. Also, the character Meg, Gideon's girlfriend, could be regarded as an allusion to Sting's actual ex-girlfriend Megan, the singer in pre-Last Exit band Earthrise. Interestingly, Meg is one part of a love triangle in the script (including Gideon and Arthur Milburn), which, according to Sting's biography, was also the case with Megan

Sting, on the stage at the Sage, during a performance of *The Last Ship*, 2015.

during the early 1970s. Perhaps the most profound resonance between the script and Sting's life is Gideon's (that is, Gordon's) determination to escape his hometown and travel the world, rebelling against the life that is plotted out for him and dreaming of an alternative future in the same way as his creator.

Embracing his Newcastle heritage in a positive way is a position that has evolved as Sting has matured, being a far cry from the antagonism he displayed when interviewed by Phil Sutcliffe in 1981 during the early years of his career.

> Sting: I don't want to be rooted in Newcastle. I don't want to be known as a Geordie. I've got none of that awful pride . . . Newcastle's a shit place. It was a slum from the Industrial Revolution and when they knocked down the old slums they built new slums.[34]

In the interview with Sutcliffe, Sting discusses how he deliberately distanced himself from his Newcastle past, deciding that 'to get on [he] had to speak in a non-accent'.[35] In a reversal of this process, over the last several years in particular, Sting has intentionally reacquainted himself with his past, realizing its importance. In many respects, Sting's wealth can be seen to distance him unavoidably from his working-class roots, leading to the understandable confusion between his actual home and an imaginary one, a factor so common in the condition known as Akenside Syndrome – 'of feeling ambivalent towards Newcastle or Tyneside despite often retaining a strong emotional bond with or sincere affection for the area'.[36] Describing a similar phenomenon, Michael Dwyer believed it to be 'not simply a romanticisation or idealisation of the comforts of home, [but rather] when the desire for homecoming is simultaneously coupled with a recognition of its impossibility'.[37] Sting has grown to recognize and use this conflict not only to give him a sense of self, but to have a positive impact on his creative work. Although he is unlikely ever to reside in Newcastle again, it is a place that unquestionably provides a sense of identity, a place he can visit both literally and figuratively via his music. It is these symbolic visitations that have encouraged Sting's creativity over the last decade. For example, on a promotional video for his *If on a Winter's Night . . .* album (2009), Sting discussed how the season of winter brought back memories of his childhood:

> Winter is the season of the imagination . . . for me. Landscapes are magically transformed by snow. I come from Wallsend on Tyne, which is very industrial, the snow would make this into a magical, magical place.[38]

Indeed, it is apparent that some of the material is not only linked to winter, but to specific places related to his youth. He saw 'The Snow It Melts the Soonest' as a reminder of 'the Northumberland moors in the winter', while 'Soul Cake' was a song he had known since he was a child.

> I knew it was a begging song, but I didn't really know the derivation of the whole thing. We did some research and we found out it was pre-Christian.[39]

It is interesting that this album followed on directly from The Police reunion tour, during which time Sting would have had to engage very much with 'the rock star side' of his personality. *If on a Winter's Night . . .* provided an opportunity once again to get back to his roots, with tracks such as 'The Snow It Melts the Soonest' grounding him in his northeast heritage. The associated DVD at Durham Cathedral was recorded in front of an invited audience, including friends and family, and the album title is based on the novel *If on a Winter's Night a Traveller* (1979) by Italo

Calvino. In the novel, Calvino positions the central character as the reader, a self-referentiality that Sting is obviously portraying when singing the eclectic collection of songs. If one listens to both the DVD and the album, it is apparent that Sting would only have recorded material such as this in late middle age, when one is more likely to look at life retrospectively. Regarding the importance of his homeland and his need to return to it, when promoting the DVD, he stated,

> I am delighted to be back here in my homeland, back to the north . . . It is fitting that I have come home in the season of the winter, because winter seems to have this almost gravitational pull to one's roots.[40]

Although Sting has sometimes been accused of disguising his Newcastle background during the early stages of his career in the late 1970s to early '80s and has accepted this accusation, it has to be stated that rock music has always been about self-invention, with numerous British artists following this trend. For example, rock vocalists such as Cliff Richard, Mick Jagger and Robert Plant sang in American accents, as did fellow Geordies such as Eric Burdon, Bryan Ferry, Jimmy Nail and Brian Johnson, but none of these artists has been accused of neglecting the 'authenticity' of his hometown background. This is because it is simply expected that rock vocalists usually sing with an American persona, so audiences are prepared to accept the allusion willingly. However, the problem Sting encountered was not related to his 'vocal persona' (which also adopted an American accent), but to his actual speaking voice – away from the music. Some of Sting's predecessors like The Beatles, Ozzy Osborne and Mick Jagger spoke in their regional accents, seemingly appearing to embrace their heritage as opposed to denying it. However, as outlined by Hugh Barker and Yuval Taylor, even some of the most 'authentic' rock musicians can be seen to be 'faking it'.[41] Most people are aware that fake names abound in popular music, but it is usually less apparent that the personas artists adopt in real life are also heavily disguised. Arguably the most famous example of this is Bob Dylan, often cited as an exemplar of authenticity, but who in reality is a bundle of disguises, including the playing down of his middle-class background and his obvious visual and musical appropriation of Woody Guthrie, who was genuinely working-class poor. Likewise, Mick Jagger and John Lennon, both of whom spoke in overt regional accents, were also, in fact, solidly middle class, prompting music journalist Caroline Coon to point out that 'Jagger spoke in a working class accent to gain credibility'.[42] Indeed, Sting's contemporary, Joe Strummer of the Clash – a band at the forefront of the punk movement, a genre so imbued with working-class ideology – was actually the son of a diplomat.[43]

The reasons Dylan, Jagger, Lennon and Strummer disguised their backgrounds and adopted working-class personas are probably related to the importance of street credibility in rock, with its antecedent, the blues, abounding in working-class artists and values. So the question is, why was Sting singled out as someone wanting to escape from his past? I would suggest that first, it has to be conceded that Sting was outspoken about his intention to distance himself from his roots. As with his comments on tantric sex, this unquestionably highlighted the issue and consequently created a story for the press, which was extended to include headlines such as 'The Police reject the north' and to reports of Sting missing his father's funeral.[44] More importantly, while the examples of Dylan, Jagger, Lennon and Strummer relate to musicians *playing down* their relatively privileged backgrounds, Sting was depicted as *playing it up*, portraying himself as middle class and arguably 'regionless', an anomaly for anyone in a punk band in the late 1970s. While race is at the centre of America's political narrative, it is class that is highlighted in the UK. By overtly disregarding his working-class past, Sting was in many ways accentuating upward social mobility, which was not part of punk's narrative and certainly not part of the ideology of the northeast of England, which is firmly regarded as a working-class area.

However, although Dylan and the others adopted distinctly working-class personas, Sting has more in common with these artists than is suggested on the surface, as they all embrace a 'real life' persona that is distinct from their background. In Sting's case, this facilitated the perception of him in a particular way, negating the often-crass and inaccurate stereotypes associated with a 'working-class Geordie'. Although it was in the interest of bands such as The Clash and The Sex Pistols to accentuate a working-class ideology because of the dystopian message they performed, this was not the case for The Police, who were not as explicitly political and were far more radio-friendly.

As Sting's public persona developed, particularly in America, it was obviously deemed important for him to appear as what John Hedley described as 'a wizard from outer space that just appeared at our doorstep'.[45] Hedley explained the development of Sting's public persona as a marketing ploy, in which '[Sting's management] tried to airbrush his background'.[46] Once this persona was established, it then became possible to engage with Sting's long-term career, free from the cultural constraints and associated expectations of his Geordie background. Although these positions are understandable in terms of career development and are common in the history of popular music going back to the blues, they are also the reasons Sting experienced criticism of the authenticity of his 'Geordieness'.

Today, despite his superstar status, Sting has evolved very much into an approachable everyman, who is regularly photographed with fans and has associations ranging from old friends in Newcastle to the social elite. Though very much a world citizen, he is also now overtly proud of his past, a reconciliation that has to be considered the main source of his creativity in recent years. Indeed, Sting's creativity and relationship with his hometown appear to be embraced in a symbiotic union, each feeding the other the necessary conditions to prosper. Having lived outside Newcastle since early 1977, Sting's perspective on his hometown can realistically be nothing but mythical and poetic, but it is this 'imaginary North' that continues to exert a gravitational pull on him. This North is refracted through separation, wealth, loss, travel and all that Sting has experienced over the last four decades. It is this North that he calls home.

While the final editing stages of this book were being undertaken, Sting announced the imminent release of *57th and 9th*, his first rock album since *Sacred Love* in 2003, named after a two-way intersection in New York that he crosses while walking from home to the recording studio. Despite the rock style of the album and its relatively delocalized narrative compared to *The Last Ship*, Sting is still engaging in the nostalgia of time and place. In addition to the occasional stylistic similarity to The Police, subjects range from global warming in 'One Fine Day', his route from Newcastle to London in 'Heading South on the Great North Road' and the refugee crisis in 'Inshalah', to the recent passing of members of his 'rock star peer group' – cultural icons such as David Bowie, Prince, Lemmy and Glen Frey. Referring to the song '50,000', he commented, 'mortality does tend to rear its head, in particular at my age . . . [so] hubris doesn't mean anything in the end.'[47] Discussing the commercial potential of the album, Sting also contextualizes it nostalgically, having been quoted as saying that he was 'keeping his expectations in check', due to rock and roll being a traditional music form as opposed to 'socially cohesive like it used to be'.[48] Considering the speed with which the album has emerged after his work on *The Last Ship*, it appears that once again, as during the four-year period leading up to *The Soul Cages* (1991), engagement with his hometown has fuelled his creativity.

CHRONOLOGY

2 October 1951

Gordon Matthew Sumner, aka Sting, is born to Ernest Matthew and Audrey Sumner. He is recorded as living at 80 Station Road, Wallsend.

1953

Sting's family is recorded as living at 35 Gerald Street, Wallsend.

1955

Sting's family is recorded as living at 84 Station Road, Wallsend, next door to number 80.

1958

Sting starts at St Columba's Infant School, Wallsend.

1963

Sting starts at St Cuthbert's Grammar School, Newcastle.

1967

Sting's family moves from Wallsend to Tynemouth. He goes to see Jimi Hendrix at the Club A'GoGo in Newcastle.

1969

The then-largest ship in the world, the *Esso Northumbria* is launched by Princess Anne at the Swan Hunter shipyard, Wallsend.

1970

Sting leaves school with A Levels in English Literature, Geography and Economics. He attends Warwick University in Coventry for a term and then works for a short time as a bus conductor.

1971

Sting commences at Northern Counties Teacher Training College in Newcastle upon Tyne. He joins Gerry Richardson's band Earthrise.

1972

Sting joins the Newcastle Big Band and the Phoenix Jazzmen.

1973

Sting records 'I'm the King of the Swingers'/'Beale Street Blues' single with the Phoenix Jazzmen at Impulse Sound Recording Studio, Wallsend.

1974

The Newcastle Big Band album is released, featuring Sting on bass.

6 June 1974

Sting commences a ten-week run of *Joseph and the Amazing Technicolor Dreamcoat* at Newcastle University Theatre.

September 1974

Sting commences teaching at St Paul's First School, Dudley Lane, Cramlington.

4 October 1974

Last Exit have their first rehearsal at the Coach Lane Campus of Northern Counties Teacher Training College, Newcastle.

16 October 1974

Last Exit begin a weekly Wednesday evening residency upstairs at The Gosforth Hotel.

December 1974

Sting performs in the Tony Hatch musical *Rock Nativity* at Newcastle University Theatre.

January 1975

Last Exit continue to perform in *Rock Nativity*.

23 February 1975

Last Exit record the Sting song 'I Got It Made' at Impulse, Wallsend.

7 March 1975

Last Exit record the Gerry Richardson song 'I'm on this Train' at Impulse Sound Recording Studio, Wallsend.

8 March 1975

Last Exit perform in local heats of the Melody Maker Battle of the Bands at Newcastle Polytechnic.

3 April 1975

Last Exit record the Sting song 'O My God' at Impulse, Wallsend.

18 April 1975

Last Exit support The Steve Brown Band at Newcastle University Theatre Bar.

21 June 1975

Last Exit support The Steve Brown Band at Tynemouth Priory.

July 1975

Last Exit 'release' a demo cassette of Impulse Sound Recording Studio recordings, entitled *A First from Last Exit*.

23 July 1975

Last Exit perform in the amateur section of the San Sebastian Jazz Festival.

26 July–5 August 1975

After playing in and winning the final of the San Sebastian Jazz Festival amateur band competition, Last Exit spend time exiled in Algorta, Spain, performing occasionally to pay their fare home.

5 October 1975

The shared residency with The Steve Brown Band and the Newcastle Big Band commences at Newcastle University Theatre Bar.

26 October 1975

Last Exit support 'The Orchestral Tubular Bells', conducted by David Bedford, featuring Andy Summers on guitar.

November 1975

Last Exit release the single 'Whispering Voices' on the Impulse Sound Recording Studio label Wudwink.

December 1975

Alongside fellow members of Last Exit, Sting performs in the musical *Hellfire* at Newcastle University Theatre.

27 April 1976

Last Exit attend their first visit to Pathway Studios in London.

28 April 1976

Last Exit are offered a deal with Virgin Publishing.

1 May 1976

Sting marries actress Frances Tomelty at the Roman Catholic Church of Our Lady and St Oswin, Front Street, Tynemouth. He begins to make weekend trips to London.

6 May 1976

Last Exit Support The Steve Brown Band at the Voom Voom Rooms, Newcastle.

23 June 1976

Last Exit support Alan Price at Newcastle City Hall as part of the Newcastle Festival, attended by Richard Branson and Carol Wilson from Virgin Records.

July 1976

Sting leaves his job as a schoolteacher.

21–4 September 1976

Following a gig at Dingwalls in London, Last Exit undertake a three-day recording session at Pathway, recording around thirteen tracks.

25 September 1976

Sting is introduced to Stewart Copeland after a Last Exit performance at St Mary's College, Newcastle.

6 November 1976

Stewart Copeland meets Andy Summers for the first time at the Drogenhayer Hotel in Newcastle.

12 November 1976

Last Exit perform at the London School of Economics.

22 November 1976

Last Exit perform live at the Newton Park Hotel in Newcastle.

23 November 1976

Sting's son Joe is born.

3 December 1976

Last Exit perform at Newcastle University Theatre Bar.

17 December 1976

According to Stewart Copeland's diary, Sting visits Stewart Copeland for a jam in London.

18 December 1976

Last Exit perform at the Nashville Room.

6 January 1977

Last Exit play their farewell performance at Newcastle University Theatre Bar.

7 January 1977

Sting and Last Exit undertake their first and only TV appearance on *The Geordie Scene*, performing 'Don't Give Up on your Daytime Job'.

8 January 1977

Sting Moves to London and reacquaints himself with Stewart Copeland the following day.

23 January 1977

The photo shoot for the cover of what would become 'Fall Out' takes place on the roof of Stewart Copeland's flat in Mayfair.

January–February 1977

Last Exit perform other London concerts, including at The Nashville Room (21 January), at the London School of Economics (22 January) and at The Red Cow (27 February).

12 February 1977

The Police record their first single 'Fall Out' at Pathway. Sting moves in to flat 2, 28a Leinster Square, Bayswater, London, where he writes many of The Police's early songs.

1 March 1977

The Police (with Henry Padovani) perform their first gig at Alexandria, Newport, Wales as part of a UK/European tour supporting Cherry Vanilla, Johnny Thunders and the Heartbreakers, Wayne County and the Electric Chairs, and Eberhard Schoener.

1 May 1977

The first single by The Police, 'Fall Out', is released.

28 May 1977

Strontium 90 perform at the Gong reunion at the Hippodrome in Paris.

31 May 1977

The Police perform their first headline gig at The Railway Hotel in London.

21 July 1977

Strontium 90 perform at The Nashville Room in London with a new name: The Elevators.

25 July 1977

The Police featuring both Andy Summers and Henry Padovani perform at The Music Machine in London, followed by a performance at Mont de Marsan in France on 5 August.

10 August 1977

The Police, with both Andy Summers and Henry Padovani, return to Pathway Studios to record a demo of 'Dead End Job' and two versions of 'Visions of the Night'.

18 August 1977

The definitive line-up of The Police performs their first concert – at Rebecca's in Birmingham.

December 1977

Introduced by Phil Sutcliffe, Last Exit Perform a one-off reunion gig at Newcastle University Theatre Bar.

January–June 1978

Interspersed with UK gigs, The Police's first album, *Outlandos d'Amour*, is recorded at Surrey Sound Studios.

15 February 1978

Sting and fellow Police members record a TV advert for Wrigley's Spearmint Gum.

April 1978

'Roxanne' is released in the UK, but does not chart.

July–August 1978

Sting is cast in *The Great Rock and Roll Swindle*.

September 1978

Sting begins filming *Quadrophenia*.

2 October 1978

The Police Perform on the BBC's *The Old Grey Whistle Test*.

20 October 1978

The Police begin their first (budget) American tour, beginning and ending with two nights at CBGBs in New York.

November 1978

Outlandos d'Amour is released in the UK. The Police's first U.S. tour finishes, closely followed by a UK tour from 23 November to 19 December.

January–February 1979

Sting plays a minor part in the road movie *Radio On*.

February–August 1979

The Police record their second album at Surrey Sound – *Reggatta de Blanc*.

21 February 1979

The Police Perform on the BBC programme *Rock Goes to College* live at Hatfield Polytechnic.

1 March–9 April 1979

The Police begin their second American tour (lasting forty days) with six performances over three days at the Whisky a Go Go in Los Angeles, CA.

6 April 1979

Outlandos d'Amour peaks at number two in the UK charts. 'Roxanne' peaks at number 32 in the Billboard Top 100.

27 April–25 May 1979

The Police return for their third tour of America, lasting 29 days.

May 1979

The re-release of 'Roxanne' peaks at number twelve in the UK charts.

31 May–24 June 1979

The Police undertake a tour of the UK, the Netherlands, Belgium and Germany.

August 1979

The re-release of 'Can't Stand Losing You' reaches number two in the UK charts.

24 August 1979

The Police headline the first day of Reading Festival. The re-release of 'Can't Stand Losing You' reaches number ten in the UK charts.

1–23 September 1979

The Police undertake a tour of Germany and the UK, culminating in two gigs at the Hammersmith Odeon.

14 September 1979

Quadrophenia is released. 'Message in a Bottle' becomes the first UK number one for The Police.

27 September–1 December 1979

The Police commence their fourth American tour (lasting 66 days), with three nights at the Grand Ballroom in New York.

2 October 1979

Reggatta de Blanc is released.

3–22 December 1979

The Police undertake another European tour, with four of the last five dates in London. 'Walking on the Moon' reaches number one in the UK.

1980

The Police tour extensively throughout the world, performing not only in Europe and North America, but in Japan, Australia, India, Egypt, Greece and Argentina.

March 1980

Sting becomes a director of Roxanne Music, to manage his performance royalties.

April 1980

Sting forms the philanthropic trust Outlandos, fronted by conservative MP Anthony Sheen. The Police perform two gigs in Newcastle with funds allocated for youth projects.

June 1980

Sting moves to Ireland for income tax reasons.

July 1980

The Police begin recording *Zenyatta Mondatta* in Hilversum, south of Amsterdam.

September 1980

'Don't Stand So Close to Me' reaches number one in the UK.

1981

The Police continue to tour not only 'major' territories, but Venezuela and Brazil.

9–12 September 1981

Sting performs 'Message in a Bottle' and 'Roxanne' at The Secret Policeman's Other Ball concerts at the Drury Lane Theatre in London in support of Amnesty International.

October 1981

'Every Little Thing She Does Is Magic' reaches number one in the UK.

November 1982

Brimstone and Treacle is released.

May 1983

'Every Breath You Take' reaches number one in the UK.

18 August 1983

The Police perform at Shea Stadium.

December 1984

Dune is released.

1985

Sting performs some early pre-release shows promoting *The Dream of the Blue Turtles* between 25 January (at the Ritz Club in New York) and 22–31 May (at the Mogador Theatre in Paris). *The Bride* is released.

1 June 1985

Sting releases his first solo album, *The Dream of the Blue Turtles*.

13 July 1985

Sting performs at Live Aid, Wembley Stadium.

10 August 1985

The Dream of the Blue Turtles tour commences in Tokyo, culminating in three dates as part of the 'Conspiracy of Hope' tour.

September 1985

Plenty is released.

4–15 June 1986

The 'Conspiracy of Hope' tour takes place.

March–August 1987

Sting Records . . . *Nothing Like the Sun*.

30 June 1987

Sting's mother dies.

August 1987

Sting works in Newcastle on *Stormy Monday*.

13 October 1987

. . . *Nothing Like the Sun* is released.

16 October 1987

. . . *Nothing Like the Sun* tour commences at the Palladium, New York. The album reaches number one in the UK.

19 November 1987

Sting's father dies.

February 1988

Julia and Julia is released.

May 1988

Stormy Monday is released.

2 September–15 October 1988

Sting takes part in the Human Rights Now! concerts.

1989

Sting establishes the Rainforest Foundation.

20 October–21 November 1989

Sting completes the final stage of the . . . *Nothing Like the Sun* tour.

1 February 1991

Sting commences *The Soul Cages* tour at Berkeley Community Theatre, San Francisco. The album reaches number one on both sides of the Atlantic.

15 February 1992

The Soul Cages tour finishes.

20 August 1992

Sting marries Trudie Styler and purchases his Lake House mansion in Wiltshire.

12 March 1993

The *Ten Summoner's Tales* tour commences, officially ending on 22 June 1995.

2 March 1996

The *Mercury Falling* tour commences, officially ending on 13 July 1997.

1999

Sting purchases the Il Palagio estate in Tuscany, Italy.

14 October 1999

The *Brand New Day* tour commences, officially ending on 14 December 2001.

2003

The Police get inducted into the Rock & Roll Hall of Fame.

12 September 2003

The *Sacred Love* tour commences, officially ending on 13 February 2005.

6 May 2006

Sting receives an honorary doctorate from Newcastle University.

3 October 2006

The *Songs from the Labyrinth* tour commences, officially ending on 11 February 2009.

2007

After a dress rehearsal on 12 February, The Police reunion tour commences on 27 May, officially ending on 7 August 2008.

19 May 2009

The *Symphonicity* tour commences, officially ending on 11 July 2011.

October 2011

Brian Yorkey workshops early scripts of *The Last Ship* in New York. Sting's Back to Bass tour commences, officially ending on 15 December 2012.

3–4 February 2012

Sting workshops *The Last Ship* at Live Theatre on Newcastle's Quayside.

25 September–9 October 2013

Sting performs eleven benefit concerts of *The Last Ship* at the Anspacher Theatre, New York.

29 September 2014

The Last Ship commences a month of previews at the Neil Simon Theatre, New York.

26 October 2014–24 January 2015

The Last Ship is performed at the Neil Simon Theatre.

24–5 April 2015

Sting brings *The Last Ship* home to Newcastle at the Sage in Gateshead.

November 2016

57th and 9th is released.

REFERENCES

INTRODUCTION

1 Christopher Sandford, *Sting: Demolition Man* (New York, 1998) and Wensley Clarkson, *The Secret Life of Gordon Sumner* (London, 1996).

2 George Lipsitz, *Dangerous Crossroads: Popular Music, Postmodernism and the Poetics of Place* (London, 1994), p. 90.

3 Philip Tagg, *Music's Meanings: A Modern Musicology for Non Musos* (New York, 2013), p. 306.

4 *The Dream of the Blue Turtles* (1985); *The Soul Cages* (1991); and *Brand New Day* (1999).

5 Sting in conversation with the author, 25 April 2015.

1 EARLY YEARS

1 The hospital where Sting was born is Grade-II listed by Historic England and part of Wallsend Hall, for many years the most imposing and impressive home in the area, occupied by the wealthiest residents of Wallsend. The last person to own the house was Sir George Burton Hunter, the owner of the Swan Hunter shipyard and Mayor of Wallsend in 1902–3. He donated the building to Wallsend Borough Council in 1916 to be used in the future as a hospital, which now bears his name – the Sir G. B. Hunter Memorial Hospital. It is interesting to note that if the building were to become a private home again, Sting is possibly the only living person to come from Wallsend who could afford it. The reason for Sting's mother not being included on the electoral register was because she was under 21 years of age, so at that point too young to vote. It was not until 1969 that the voting age was reduced from 21 to eighteen. The author would like to thank Ken Hutchinson for these observations, in addition to many others in this chapter.

2 Sting, *Broken Music* (London, 2003), p. 30.

3 Ibid.

4 Ibid.

5 Ibid., p. 31.

6 Ibid., p. 25.

7 Hutchinson, in email conversation with the author, 17 October 2014.

8 Sting, *Broken Music*, p. 30.

9 This was the point at which Sting and his parents would have been living at number 80 with Amy Foster.

10 Wensley Clarkson, *The Secret Life of Gordon Sumner* (London, 1996), p. 2.

11 Hutchinson proceeded to describe the flat in Gerald Street as follows: '35 Gerald Street was a typical "Tyneside Flat", a unique form of housing built all over Tyneside to house shipyard workers and other working men. Instead of the traditional terrace of houses usually built for workers, the Tyneside flat had two adjoining front doors leading to separate flats, one on the ground floor and one on the first floor separated horizontally. The back garden was divided into two, vertically, with two back gates leading onto the back lane. At the end of the yard was the outside toilet for each flat.' Hutchinson in email conversation with the author, 18 July 2014.

12 Sting, *Broken Music*, pp. 27, 49.

13 Ibid., p. 49.

14 Ibid., p. 18.

15 Ibid., p. 29. All three of Sting's early homes would have been without central heating.

16 Anthony Decurtis, 'The Healing Power of Music' (7 February 1991), www.sting.com, accessed 30 April 2017.

17 N.A., 'Rock Star Sting Unveils Artwork of Geordie Roots', *Evening Chronicle* (31 October 2000), www.chroniclelive.co.uk, accessed 14 January 2015.

18 Sting, *Broken Music*, p. 35.

19 Built by Emperor Hadrian (AD 76–138), the 118-km- (73-mile-) long World Heritage Site progresses westerly from Wallsend to Bowness-on-Solway, a small village on the borders of England and Scotland. However, the history of the area goes back a lot further than the Roman occupation, *Segedunum* being a Latinization of a Brythonic (proto-Welsh) name, probably meaning 'dry hill' (cf. *Sychdyn*).

20 Sting, *Broken Music*, p. 26.

21 David Bryne, 'What Sort of Future?', in *Geordies: Roots of Regionalism*, ed. Robert Colls and Bill Lancaster (Edinburgh, 1992), p. 36.

22 'Sting: Fields of Gold, CD Digipack', www.sting.com, accessed 27 January

2015. The first pit shaft to be sunk in Wallsend in 1778 was close to *Segedunum* Roman Fort and actually on the site later developed as Gerald Street.

23 Sting alludes to the dangers of the shipbuilding industry in his song 'Island of Souls' from the *Soul Cages*.

24 Sting, *Broken Music*, pp. 67, 69.

25 Ibid., p. 69.

26 Ibid.

27 Ibid., p. 73.

28 Ibid., p. 74.

29 Tony Bianchi in conversation with the author, 8 July 2014.

30 Ibid.

31 Ibid.

32 Ibid.

33 Ibid. For an amusing, albeit also slightly mythologized, account of Sting's time at St Cuthbert's School, see James Berryman, *Sting and I: The Totally Hilarious Story of Life as Sting's Best Mate* (London, 2005).

34 E. J. Hobsbawm and T. O. Ranger, *The Invention of Tradition* (Cambridge, 1983), p. 96.

35 Sting, *Broken Music*, p. 90.

36 There is also a category of musician who simply adopts a single-word stage name in order to be successful in show business. Artists such as Lulu, Seal, Dido, Eminem and Ludacris are indicative examples. This can easily be extended by including artists who base stage names on their surnames (for example, Liberace), middle names (such as Rihanna) or forenames (Beck, Madonna, Shakira, Usher, Prince and Björk). These tendencies are distinct from artists who have adopted double-barrelled persona stage names. This is a phenomenon that arguably commenced with artists such as Leadbelly, Tampa Red and Muddy Waters, before progressing to more contemporary examples such as Engelbert Humperdinck, Elton John, David Bowie, Cat Stephens, Lady Gaga, etc.

2 MAN IN A SUITCASE

1 Sting, *Broken Music* (London, 2003), p. 26.

2 Michael Jackson and Prince, for example, were both inherently shy but extroverted performers under the guise of their personas.

3 Robert Colls and Bill Lancaster, eds, *Geordies: Roots of Regionalism* (Edinburgh, 1992), p. xii.

4 Ibid.

5 Christopher Sandford, *Sting: Demolition Man* (New York, 1998), p. 8, and Wensley Clarkson, *The Secret Life of Gordon Sumner: Sting* (London, 1996), p. 1.

6 Colls and Lancaster, *Geordies: Roots of Regionalism*, p. xiv.

7 See Barbara Hodgson, 'Amazing News for Gateshead Online Music Company as it Launches in America', *The Journal*, 23 May 2014, www.thejournal.co.uk, accessed 16 July 2015. Other examples of Sting's ties to his home city include the following: 1) a painting of the river Tyne owned by Sting is currently housed at Newcastle's Laing Art Gallery. Painted by Academy-Award-winner Stephen Hannock and entitled *Northern City Renaissance, Newcastle England*, the work depicts a contemporary Newcastle on the surface, including landmarks such as the Sage and Millennium Bridge. Partially hidden under the surface are images and text relating to Newcastle's mining heritage; 2) Sting received an honorary doctorate from Newcastle University on 5 May 2006; 3) In May 2004 Sting performed with ex-Last Exit keyboard player Gerry Richardson's band at Newcastle Civic Centre, when being honoured by The Variety Club of Great Britain (receiving the 'Silver Heart'). During the concert, two students from Newcastle College also performed with Sting's band on stage; 4) The embryonic performances of *The Last Ship* were performed at the Live Theatre in Newcastle, during which he performed drafts of the songs and ran the concept past an invited audience; 5) The movie *Stormy Monday* (1988), starring Sting, was set in Newcastle.

8 Vic Garbarini, *Bass Player* (1 April 1992), www.sting.com, accessed 30 April 2017.

9 Sting, *Lyrics by Sting* (London, 2007), p. 144. Sting's father, in fact, died in 1987, so this date is obviously a typographical error.

10 Anthony Decurtis, 'Sting: New Album Brings Renewed Perspective', *Rolling Stone* (7 February 1991), www.rollingstone.com, accessed 7 September 2015.

11 Jon Pareles, 'Taking Himself Out of the Equation: Sting Frees Himself with the Writing of *The Last Ship*', *New York Times* (12 September 2013), www.nytimes.com.

12 Sting, 'How I Started Writing Songs Again' [video], TED 2014, March 2014, www.ted.com.

13 Ibid.

14 Dave Russell, *Looking North: Northern England and the National Imagination* (Manchester, 2004), p. 4.

15 *Billy Elliot* is based on the strikes of the coal-mining industry of the northeast during the mid-1980s.

16 Russell, *Looking North: Northern England and the National Imagination*, p. 7.

17 Robert Colls, 'Born-again Geordies', in *Geordies: Roots of Regionalism,*
    ed. Robert Colls and Bill Lancaster (Edinburgh, 1992), p. 14.
18 Ibid.
19 *The Stars Look Down* has a subplot of upward mobility, the need to move to
    London to achieve this and the lack of understanding by the older generation
    regarding the need to escape. A similar process can be seen in the film *How
    Green Was My Valley* of 1941, which, although set in the coal mines of Wales,
    was actually shot in the United States.
20 Colls, 'Born-again Geordies', p. 17.
21 Previews of *The Last Ship* started on Broadway on 29 September 2014.
22 Raymond MacDonald, David Hargreaves and Dorothy Miell, *Musical Identities*
    (Oxford, 2002), p. 10.
23 John Hedley in conversation with the author, 12 June 2014.
24 Interview with Lauren Laverne, *The Culture Show*, 26 November 2009 (BBC
    Two).
25 Ibid.
26 Paul Du Noyer, 'Stingtime in Paris: The Police Chief Sets Himself Free',
    New Musical Express (1 June 1985), www.sting.com, accessed 30 April 2017.
27 Ibid.
28 Ibid.
29 Ibid.
30 Sting's narration of Prokofiev's *Peter and the Wolf* (1991) and Stravinsky's
    The Soldier's Tale (1988) are examples of his interface with classical music.
    He also recorded orchestral versions of his songs on *Symphonicities* (2010).
    The albums . . . *Nothing Like the Sun* (1987) and *The Soul Cages* (1991) were
    dedicated to his mother and father, respectively. It could be argued that
    Sting's work on *The Last Ship* is an extension of the Tin Pan Alley tradition,
    in which there was a clear separation between performer and songwriter;
    more accustomed to being the 'star persona', this is an unusual position for
    Sting.
31 Nicholas Cook, *Music: A Very Short Introduction* (Oxford, 2000), p. 11.
32 Kristine McKenna, 'A Monster Called Sting', *Rolling Stone*, 403 (1 September
    1983), pp. 15–18.
33 Sting, *Bring on the Night* [DVD], A&M Films, 1985.
34 Gay Rosenthal, 'Sting Behind the Music' [video], 26 September 1999, available
    at YouTube, www.youtube.com, accessed 30 April 2017.
35 Ibid.
36 Ibid.
37 See Sting's iPad application, *Sting 25 Years* (2013).

38 Tom Cochrane, Bernardino Fantini and Klaus Scherer, *The Emotional Power of Music: Multidisciplinary Perspectives on Musical Arousal, Expression, and Social Control* (Oxford, 2013), p. 24.

39 These are essentially characters in the song that are neither real people nor the personae. In *The Republic*, Plato distinguishes between what he describes as *diegesis*, describing a narrator speaking as himself, and *mimesis*, which describes a narrator speaking as a character or not as himself. For a discussion of how musicologist Allan Moore has adapted this terminology, see Allan Moore, *Rock: The Primary Text – Developing a Musicology of Rock* (London, 2013), p. 181.

40 George Lipsitz describes this process as 'strategic anti-essentialist'. See George Lipsitz, *Dangerous Crossroads: Popular Music, Postmodernism and the Poetics of Place* (New York, 1994), p. 62.

41 Caroline Sullivan, 'Sting: *The Last Ship* – Review', *The Guardian* (20 September 2013), p. 24.

42 'Sting and Jimmy Nail on Creating *The Last Ship* Album' [video], BBC, www.bbc.co.uk, accessed 7 July 2015.

43 Philip Norman, 'Sting and The Police: The Rhetoric of Stardom', *Sunday Times* (1981), available at www.rocksbackpages.com, accessed 30 April 2017.

44 Chris Salewicz, 'Sting: Coming Home', *Time Out* (1982), available at www.rocksbackpages.com, accessed 30 April 2017. Salewicz is referring to the Viking roots of the northeast of England.

45 Salewicz, 'Sting: Coming Home'.

46 Ibid.

47 The allusion to folk music via instruments such as the Northumbrian pipes can result in feelings such as nostalgia, pride or melancholy (specifically, a hankering for one's homeland). In addition to symbolizing specific places, sounds such as these can also result in a feeling of timelessness. For example, although 'Island of Souls' from *The Soul Cages* was written in the early 1990s, the Northumbrian pipes could have sounded decades, or even hundreds of years, prior to this. This can give the music a universality that moves beyond specific recordings, places and spaces.

3 LAST EXIT

1 Sting, *Broken Music* (London, 2003), p. 101.

2 Gerry Richardson, 'A Brief History of Last Exit', in *All Right Now: A Brief History of Newcastle*, ed. Anna Flowers and Vanessa Histon (Newcastle, 2011), pp. 66–8.

3 Ibid.
4 The official title of 'I'm the King of the Swingers' is 'I Wan'na Be Like You (The Monkey Song)'.
5 *Newcastle Big Band*, Wudwink/Impulse Organisation (is-nbb-106, no date). As there is no date on the album, there is much debate regarding when the album was recorded and released. Although a number of websites give 1972 as the release date, saxophonist Lance Liddle, who played with the big band up until 1973, confirmed that the album was released after he left.
6 The Newcastle University Theatre Bar is now called the Northern Stage.
7 Sting, *Broken Music*, p. 116.
8 Ibid.
9 Although the date of this is not explicit in Sting's autobiography *Broken Music*, he does recall having auditions for the Newcastle Big Band after 'Gerry [Richardson] leaves for Bristol', p. 114. Having met Richardson in 1971 and worked with him for a year prior to Richardson's departure, it is estimated, in 1972.
10 Andy Hudson in conversation with the author, 6 July 2015.
11 Ibid.
12 Ibid.
13 Sting, *Broken Music*, p. 178.
14 Hedley had played on the band's only album – *Brian Davidson's Every Which Way* (1970).
15 John Hedley in conversation with the author, 12 June 2014.
16 Ibid.
17 Sting, *Broken Music*, p. 85.
18 James Berryman, *Sting and I: The Totally Hilarious Story of Life as Sting's Best Mate* (London, 2005). Sting refutes this in his autobiography.
19 Hedley in conversation with the author.
20 Ibid.
21 Sting, *Broken Music*, p. 170. According to John Hedley, after an altercation with the band's roadies, Last Exit were left stranded in Spain. They were fortunate to receive accommodation in return for a gig at the Algorta Jazz Festival on Saturday 3 August 1975. During their stay, they also performed a few gigs in and around Bilbao to raise money for their return journey home.
22 Sting, *Broken Music*, p. 127.
23 Ibid., p. 100.
24 David Whetstone, 'Sting Talks About His New Album and Stage Show', *The Journal* (20 September 2013), www.thejournal.co.uk.
25 Sting, *Broken Music*, p. 139.

26 Sting met his first wife Frances Tomelty during this season of performances. Tomelty was a key figure in facilitating Sting's move to London in the early months of 1977.

27 Whetstone, 'Sting Talks About his New Album and Stage Show'.

28 Sting, *Broken Music*, p. 152.

29 'Last Exit: First From Last Exit', www.sting.com, accessed 15 January 2015. This information is taken from Dave Dunn and Wendy Dunn, 'A Rough Guide to Last Exit', *The Outlandos Fan Club Spring 2001 Newsletter*, pp. 23–7.

30 Phil Sutcliffe in conversation with the author, 6 March 2015.

31 Sid Smith in conversation with the author, 13 July 2015.

32 Richardson, 'A Brief History of Last Exit'.

33 Ibid.

34 Gerry Richardson in conversation with the author, 2 July 2014.

35 Phil Sutcliffe in conversation with the author, 6 March 2015.

36 Sting, *Broken Music*, p. 185.

37 Smith in conversation with the author.

38 EmCee Five, *Bebop 61* (Birdland, 1967).

39 Smith in conversation with the author.

40 Ibid.

41 Ibid.

42 Phil Sutcliffe and Hugh Fielder, *L'Historia Bandido* (New York, 1981).

43 Richardson, 'A Brief History of Last Exit'.

44 Jeffrey the Barak in conversation with the author.

45 Ibid.

46 Smith in conversation with the author.

47 These events were organized as part of an A&R 'showcase'. Although the performance did not result in a record contract, Last Exit did secure a publishing deal with Virgin.

48 Peter Smith, 'Last Exit Newcastle 1975', https://vintagerock.wordpress.com, accessed 15 January 2015.

49 Andy Summers, *One Train Later* (New York, 2006), p. 166.

50 This is confirmed in John Hedley's diary, which outlined a number of performances at the Lion Inn at Blakey Ridge, a pub on the north Yorkshire Moors made famous by Back Door. Last Exit's final performance at the venue prior to their Newcastle City Hall performance was on Tuesday 2 September 1975, and they were paid £4 each.

51 His last gig is reported to be at the Gosforth Hotel, on Wednesday 29 October 1975.

52 John Hedley in conversation with the author, 12 June 2014.

53 Ibid.

54 Ibid. Hedley had, in fact, already left the band by the time Last Exit performed at Dingwalls.

55 Phil Sutcliffe, 'Making It: Last Exit' (8 January 1977), www.rocksbackpages. com, accessed 30 April 2017.

56 Sutcliffe in conversation with the author.

57 'Apathy Hitting North Music', *Evening Chronicle* (13 March 1975), p. 14.

58 Ibid.

59 The album was eventually re-released by Warner Brothers.

60 Sid Smith, 'Sting and Last Exit', http://sidsmith.blogspot.co.uk, accessed 15 January 2015.

4 EARLY RECORDINGS

1 David Wood in conversation with the author, 12 June 2014.

2 Mickey Sweeney in conversation with the author, 2 April 2014.

3 Ibid.

4 Ibid.

5 Ibid.

6 Ibid.

7 Ibid.

8 Gerry Richardson in conversation with the author, 2 July 2014.

9 John Hedley in conversation with the author, 12 June 2014.

10 Wood in conversation with the author.

11 Hedley in conversation with the author.

12 Ibid.

13 Sting, *Broken Music* (London, 2003), p. 167.

14 As Sting was working with the Synclavier by this point, the likelihood is that the demo was recorded using this device.

15 Keith Nichol in conversation with the author, 1 April 2014.

16 Ibid.

17 This includes recordings supplied by Impulse owner David Wood and the Last Exit bootleg CD, *Sting Last Exit Impulse Studio Demos*, 2014 (although many of the recordings on this CD were not recorded at Impulse).

18 Sting, *Broken Music*, p. 185.

19 'Last Exit: First from Last Exit' (2001), www.sting.com, accessed 20 January 2015.

20 Both 'O My God' and 'I'm on this Train' were subsequently re-recorded at Pathway.

21 This is confirmed in Phil Sutcliffe's article in *Sounds*, which recounts the band recording their first demo while performing in Rock Nativity towards the end of 1974. See Phil Sutcliffe 'Making It: Last Exit' (8 January 1977), www.rocksbackpages.com, accessed 30 April 2017.

22 The cassette included an alternative, slightly longer version of 'Whispering Voices' to that recorded on the later *A First from Last Exit* cassette.

23 This track is actually entitled 'A Bit of *Piece*' on the Pathway cover, but it is presumed this is simply a spelling mistake.

24 'I'm on this Train' features Ronnie Pearson on lead vocals in the verse, with Sting taking over in the chorus, while 'Whispering Voices' is sung by drummer Ronnie Pearson.

25 Sutcliffe, 'Making It: Last Exit'.

26 Tony Harris in email conversation with the author, 7 February 2015.

27 Sting, *Broken Music*, p. 184.

28 Ibid., p. 185.

29 Last Exit, *Sting Last Exit Impulse Studio Demos*, 2014.

30 'Night at the Grand Hotel' includes 'Rocky Horror'-style vocal overdubs. 'Savage Beast' and 'Don't You Look at Me' shift between overdubbed acoustic and electric guitar. 'Fool in Love' appears to feature Sting singing backing vocals to his own lead vocal.

31 Phil Sutcliffe and Hugh Fielder, *L'Historia Bandido* (New York, 1981), p. 35.

32 Ibid.

33 This recording does not have any Latin American stylistic influences, but presents a selection of songs such as 'Fragile', 'They Stand Alone' and 'Little Wing' recorded in Spanish and Portuguese.

34 Sting progresses between these two types of voice in a number of ways. For example, songs such as 'Don't Stand So Close to Me' tend to move to falsetto towards the end of the song. During his years with The Police, Sting would often sing entire songs in this distinctive falsetto voice, a factor which made his vocal instantly recognizable (for example, listen to 'So Lonely', 'Roxanne' and 'Hole in My Life' from *Outlandos D'Amour*). Interestingly, songs such as 'Message in a Bottle' and 'Walking on the Moon' (from *Regatta De Blanc*) interchange between using the falsetto in the verse and Sting's chest voice for the chorus, while 'Contact' (from the same album) reverses this trend, using his chest for the verse and falsetto for the chorus.

35 The Grand Hotel in Tynemouth was a place associated with Sting's first marriage to Frances Tomelty in 1976, at St Paul's Church in nearby Whitley Bay. He recalled 'having a small gathering' (Sting, *Broken Music*, p. 188) the

night before his wedding, with a number of Tomelty's family staying in the hotel overnight. The lyrics of the song depict a 'rocky-horror'-style night in the hotel, with damp rooms and poor food.

36 Sting, *Broken Music*, p. 284.

37 This track was rearranged for *Ghost in the Machine*, but did not make the final cut. It is unclear why the song was not taken forward by The Police, but when, in email conversation with Dietmar Clös, The Police's then-guitarist Henry Padovani recalled 'Stewart [Copeland] reacting "badly" to it . . . it wasn't the sort of slogan you were supposed to sing, in those days . . . the whole point was to give it up and destroy everything along the way. (Henry Padovani in email conversation with Dietmar Clös, 28 August 2014.)

38 This track was also rearranged for *Ghost in the Machine*, but did not make the final cut.

39 Featuring acoustic guitar for the rhythm part, this song was also subsequently recorded in demo format for *Ghost in the Machine*, but never made the final cut.

40 As recorded on *The Dream of the Blue Turtles* (1985).

41 When in email conversation with Dietmar Clös, Stewart Copeland recalled the title change being his idea, 'I reckoned that truth is a good thing rather than bad. God knows what the rest of the lyric was about.' (Stewart Copeland in email conversation with Dietmar Clös, 24 July 2015.)

42 Although it was not possible to listen to the Last Exit original studio recording of 'Don't Give Up on your Daytime Job', it was possible to hear it via a live bootleg recorded towards the end of 1976 at the Gosforth Hotel.

43 A live recording of this song by The Police, featuring Henry Padovani, is available between 6:39 and 9:54 at www.youtube.com.

44 However, the final verse of 'The Bed's too Big without You' contains the phrase 'Every Day Is Just the Same'. The song 'I Can't Say' was eventually given to Rubèn Blades for his *Nothing but the Truth* album (1988).

45 Anna Maria Jopek, *Secret* (2005); Kevyn Lettau, *Walking in your Footsteps* (2003); Julienne Taylor, *Racing the Clouds Home* (2000).

46 Sting, *Broken Music*, p. 163

47 Sutcliffe and Fielder, *L'Historia Bandido*, p. 36.

48 *DubXanne* (2008).

49 Christopher Gable, *The Words and Music of Sting* (Westport, CT, 2008), p. 37.

50 Ibid.

51 Christopher Sandford, *Sting: Demolition Man* (New York, 1998).

52 These similarities are also apparent in the original version of 'We Work the Black Seam' on *The Dream of the Blue Turtles* (1984). Although this version

only has five verses, it is comprised of sections of both verses of 'Savage Beast'.

53 'Dead Man's Rope' references 'Walking in your Footsteps' from *Synchronicity*. 'We'll Be Together' references 'If You Love Somebody Set Them Free' from *The Dream of the Blue Turtles*.

54 This song was also recorded on a pre-Police album, *Strontium 90: Police Academy* (1977).

55 Guns N' Roses used the title on the *End of Days* soundtrack in 1999. The Kaiser Chiefs used the title on their album *Drowned in Sound* of 2004, while Jay-Z used the title on *Kingdom Come* (2006).

5 THE POLICE

1 Sting, *Broken Music* (London, 2003), p. 225.

2 Keyboard player Gerry Richardson did make the move to London, returning to Newcastle after working as a freelance musician for a number of years.

3 These gigs were part of a Last Exit 'mini tour', commencing in Bristol on 20 January 1977 (which, according to Sting's autobiography, was double-booked), followed by the aforementioned sequence of gigs and finishing with a one-off performance at Middlesbrough Rock Garden on 28 January.

4 Sting, *Broken Music*, p. 256.

5 An example from this time is the song 'Landlord', which was the B-side to 'Message in a Bottle' (1979).

6 Copeland spent the following day in Newcastle, attending a Last Exit performance with Sutcliffe at St Mary's College on Sunday 25 September. It was at this gig that Sting was introduced to Stewart Copeland. Sting's autobiography indicates that the meeting in Green Street was dated 9 January 1977, although Stewart Copeland's personal diary recalls Sting arriving in London for a jam on 17 December 1976. In conversation with Phil Sutcliffe, his recollection was that Copeland made the initial attempt to get in touch with Sting, calling him in Newcastle and asking for Sting's number.

7 Sting, *Broken Music*, p. 233.

8 John Covach, 'Progressive Rock, "Close to the Edge," and the Boundaries of Style', ed. John Covach and Graeme M. Boone, *Understanding Rock: Essays in Musical Analysis* (New York, 1997), p. 4.

9 Ibid., p. 5.

10 See Dick Hebdige, *Subculture: The Meaning of Style* (London, 1979), p. 109.

11 Ibid.

12 Tim Jackson, 'Chasing Progress: Beyond Measuring Economic Growth', New Economics Foundation, 2004.

13 Phil Longman, 'Was 1976 All that It was Cracked Up to Be?', BBC News (17 March 2004), http://news.bbc.co.uk.

14 Keir Mudie, '1976 was Britain's Best Ever Year According to New Study', *Daily Mirror* (21 July 2013), www.mirror.co.uk.

15 Hebdige, *Subculture: The Meaning of Style*, p. 25.

16 It has been argued that reggae as a musical movement represents the alienation of many black youths in the UK during this period, thus paralleling the frustration felt by punks.

17 Alan Jones, 'Sting: Can't Stand Losing', *Melody Maker* (22 September 1979), p. 42.

18 Although the story is anecdotal, according to Mark Spicer, Sting threw a party towards the end of 1977, for which Stewart Copeland lent him some records – including albums by Bob Marley. It was this that sparked his interest, just prior to the recording of the band's first album. See Mark Spicer, 'Reggatta de Blanc: Analysing Style in the Music of the Police', in *Sounding Out Pop: Analytical Essays in Popular Music*, ed. Mark Spicer and John Covach (Ann Arbor, MI, 2010), pp. 124–53.

19 Mike Howlett in conversation with the author, 26 November 2014.

20 Only Sting and Stewart Copeland performed as part of the Cherry Vanilla backing band.

21 Although they had recorded the single 'Fall Out' at that point, it was not released until May 1977. Jonny Perkins, *In It 4 the Crack* (Gwent, 2012), p. 53. In his autobiography, Andy Summers recalls Stewart Copeland informing him that The Police were 'backing her [Cherry Vanilla] up for fifteen quid a night', so it appears that Perkins's details are correct; see Andy Summers, *One Train Later* (New York, 2006), p. 168. Sting recalls being paid £6.50 for the gig in his autobiography (p. 255), so it appears that the £15 was divided between band members unevenly.

22 Perkins, *In It 4 the Crack*, p. 53.

23 Sting, *Broken Music*, p. 254.

24 Ibid.

25 Jonny Perkins in conversation with the author, 1 October 2014. Based on these audience figures, The Police would have played to a largely empty venue for this inaugural performance. The building, which was originally a car sales room, has subsequently been partially demolished and turned into flats.

26 Perkins in conversation with the author.

27 See Oliver Craske, *Punk Rock: An Oral History* (London, 2007), p. 260, and

Jon Savage, *England's Dreaming: The Sex Pistols and Punk Rock* (London, 1991), p. 157.

28 Perkins, *In It 4 the Crack*, p. 35.

29 Perkins also used the 'New Wave Rock' label to publicize the concerts he promoted after the closure of The Alexandria Club.

30 In his autobiography (p. 255), Sting recalls having a half-hour break between sets.

31 Perkins in conversation with the author.

32 Wensley Clarkson's book on Sting reported the set as lasting forty minutes. He also reports the name of the club as being the Stowaway Club. According to Clarkson, the set that night mainly consisted of Stewart Copeland songs. See Wensley Clarkson, *Sting: The Secret Life of Gordon Sumner* (London, 1996), p. 61; Sting, *Broken Music*, p. 255.

33 'Nothing Achieving' was the first recorded song by The Police to be penned by Sting. Padovani only played the guitar solos, while Copeland played the rhythm parts himself.

34 Pathway used a sixteen-track mixing desk into a Brennel Richardson eight-track recorder. Squeeze's debut album *Squeeze* (1978) was recorded between Pathway and the studio – Surrey Sound – where The Police were to record their first album. Dire Straits' demo version of 'Sultans of Swing' was recorded at Pathway in 1978.

35 See Polly Marshall, *The God of Hellfire: The Crazy Life and Times of Arthur Brown* (London, 2006).

36 Costello's *My Aim Is True* was recorded at Pathway between late 1976 and early 1977. The Damned debut album *Damned, Damned, Damned* was recorded at Pathway between September 1976 and January 1977, and released on 18 February 1977. This album is often credited as the first album to be released by a UK punk group. The original version of 'The Prince' by Madness was recorded in Pathway in June 1979. See John Reed, *House of Fun: The Story of 'Madness'* (London, 2011). For a comprehensive list of records recorded at Pathway, see www.philsbook.com.

37 Sting, *Broken Music*, p. 244.

38 It is interesting to compare the cover of 'Fall Out' with those of the later 'I Can't Stand Losing You' (released August '78 in the UK), 'So Lonely' (released October '78 in the UK) and 'Roxanne' (released for the second time in April '79 in the UK), all of which use black-and-white imagery.

39 The image of the three band members is far more coordinated and groomed on the covers of 'I Can't Stand Losing You', 'So Lonely' and 'Roxanne' than on 'Fall Out'. By the release of 'Roxanne' of course, the

band were attempting to appeal to a global market, had adopted their now-famous blond image and were being positioned in such a way as to place them as distinct from the anarchy of punk rock. The sharp, straight-lined font of 'The Police' band name is consistent and masculine throughout all of the band's discography, which is often contrasted with more feminine-looking fonts on 'Roxanne' and 'Walking on the Moon', not to mention their first three albums.

40 Lawrence Impey in conversation with the author, 20 February 2015.

41 Ibid.

42 Dave Laing, *One Chord Wonders: Power and Meaning in Punk Rock* (Oakland, CA, 1985), p. 27.

43 This included a performance in Sting's hometown, at Newcastle Polytechnic, on 6 May 1977. This was the first time that Sting had performed back in Newcastle since leaving Last Exit. In his autobiography, he recalls the gig being 'blown off the stage by a local group called Penetration . . . The best punk band I have ever seen' (Sting, *Broken Music*, p. 275).

44 Sting, *Broken Music*, p. 276.

45 Howlett at that point was the 'ex' bass player in Gong. During the concert, each member of Gong performed with his own group, prior to them appearing together as Gong.

46 This was subsequently released as a double album: *Gong est Mort, Vive Gong* (1977). Although Sting recounts the festival as lasting for twelve hours in his autobiography, Andy Summers remembers it as lasting eight hours in his. See Andy Summers, *One Train Later*, p. 167.

47 Sting, *Broken Music*, p. 271.

48 Mike Howlett in conversation with the author, 26 November 2014.

49 Ibid.

50 Summers, *One Train Later*, p. 168.

51 Lady June (1931–1999) was a painter, poet and musician who was closely involved with the Canterbury progressive rock scene. The flat to which Howlett is referring became a place where musicians from bands such as Gong and Soft Machine frequently used to hang out. It is also known as the place where Soft Machine's Robert Wyatt fell from a window and broke his back – an incident that occurred when Howlett was in attendance.

52 Howlett in conversation with the author.

53 Ibid.

54 Sting, *Broken Music*, p. 272.

55 Mark Spicer, 'Reggatta de Blanc', p. 129.

56 *VH1 Storytellers: Sting*, VH1 (broadcast 15 July 1996).

57　Daniel Rachel, *Isle of Noises: Conversations with Great British Songwriters* (London, 2013), p. 200.

58　For example, the opening chord of 'New World Blues' is rather 'eastern'-sounding.

59　In addition to these recordings, Sting recorded a single for an anti-nuclear campaign under the pseudonym The Radio Actors. Commencing recording at Mike Howlett's project studio in Acton before moving to Virtual Earth, the single, featuring 'Nuclear Waste' on side A and 'Digital Love' as a B-side, included musicians such as Steve Hillage and Mike Howlett, alongside the likes of Nik Turner and Steve Broughton.

60　Howlett in conversation with the author.

61　Some of these bands were also featured in *The Punk Rock Movie* (1978), much of which was recorded live at The Roxy.

62　Paul Marko, *The Roxy London wc2: A Punk History* (London, 2007), p. 2.

63　Howlett in conversation with the author.

64　Sting, *Broken Music*, p. 277.

65　The final recording is a combination of both original takes. Ex-Velvet Underground member John Cale produced this session.

66　Sting, *Broken Music*, p. 283.

67　Summers, *One Train Later*, p. 176.

68　Ibid.

69　Howlett in conversation with the author.

70　Phil Sutcliffe in conversation with the author, 6 March 2015.

71　The *Birmingham Mail* described the Fewtrell family as 'the Kings of Clubland'. See Mike Lockley, 'Fewtrell: The name Known Throughout Birmingham', www.birminghammail.co.uk, accessed 30 April 2017. The Casaba was located on the top floor and described as the more refined of the three rooms, according to a local DJ. It was possible to have a meal in this space. See Barry John (2014), 'Rebecca's – My Memories', available at www.djbarryjohn.co.uk, accessed 31 January 2015. The Blue Soul Room was on the middle floor.

72　XTC played there on 9 June, 30 June and 14 July.

6 SONGWRITING

1　Sting, *Broken Music* (London, 2003), p. 227.

2　Ibid., p. 228.

3　Ibid., p. 243.

4　Ibid., pp. 244–5.

5 Sting refers to writing the guitar riff of 'Walking on the Moon' in this flat. See Sting, *Lyrics by Sting* (London, 2007), p. 26.

6 Ibid., p. 4.

7 Sting, *Broken Music*, pp. 180–81.

8 Christopher Sandford, *Sting: Demolition Man* (New York, 1998), p. 56. This date is, however, disputed in Stewart Copeland's diary, in which he dates the event to 15 February. The author would like to thank Dietmar Clös for pointing this out.

9 Sting, *Broken Music*, p. 292.

10 Andy Summers, *One Train Later* (New York, 2006), p. 193.

11 Sting, *Broken Music*, p. 309.

12 The Police appeared on *The Old Grey Whistle Test* on Sting's 27th birthday (2 October 1978) while he was still filming the movie. His hair was still stylized to that of his character Ace Face. For a detailed account of Sting's movies and the ways in which they relate to his personality, see Phil Powrie, 'The Sting in the Tale', *Popular Music and Film*, ed. Ian Inglis (London, 2003), pp. 39–59.

13 Andy Hudson was keen to point out that the mechanics of Sting getting his Equity card in order to act in the film were complex, taking place over a weekend and involving the Musicians Union, the Variety Artists Federation and finally Equity. 'It was like a food chain, because if you were in the Musicians Union, you could also be in the Variety Artists Federation, and if you were in the Variety Artists Federation, you could also be in Equity. It resulted in him getting his Equity card' (Andy Hudson, in conversation with the author, 6 July 2015).

14 Summers, *One Train Later*, p. 229.

15 Sting, *Broken Music*, p. 292.

16 Sandford, *Sting: Demolition Man*, p. 59.

17 Ibid., p. 293. Sting added the lyrics of 'Peanuts' to Copeland's music, and 'Be My Girl – Sally' with Summers, the latter of whom wrote the 'Pythonesque' narrative in the middle of the song.

18 Sting cites it as the reason for the ultimate demise of the band. See Sting, *Broken Music*, p. 294.

19 The song may have been written during the early days of living in London.

20 Phil Sutcliffe in conversation with the author, 6 March 2015.

21 Ibid.

22 Sting, *Lyrics by Sting*, p. 7. The introduction of reggae into his repertoire on the first album is also featured on songs such as 'Hole in My Life', 'Can't Help Losing You' and 'Masoko Tanga'.

23 Sandford, *Sting: Demolition Man*, pp. 58–9.

24 Summers, *One Train Later*, p. 193.

25 Ibid., p. 190.

26 Sting, *Broken Music*, p. 195.

27 Summers, *One Train Later*, p. 189.

28 However, most of the original material came from Sting or keyboard player Gerry Richardson. John Hedley in conversation with the author, 12 June 2014, and Gerry Richardson in conversation with the author, 14 July 2014.

29 The Police, *Police in Montserrat*, BBC (broadcast 1980), available at https://vimeo.com, accessed 30 April 2017.

30 Sting, quoted in *Police in Montserrat*.

31 Ibid.

32 Stewart Copeland quoted in Mark Spicer, 'Reggata de Blanc: Analysing Style in the Music of the Police', in *Sounding Out Pop: Analytical Essays in Popular Music*, ed. Mark Spicer and John Covach (Ann Arbor, MI, 2010), p. 144.

33 Summers, *One Train Later*, p. 295.

34 Ibid.

35 Richardson in conversation with the author. Andy Summers's account is very different from this – he stated in his autobiography that he was responsible for writing the guitar riff. See Andy Summers, *One Train Later*, p. 323.

36 Richardson in conversation with the author.

37 Matthew Brown, 'Little Wing: A Study in Musical Cognition', in *Understanding Rock*, ed. John Covach and Graeme M. Boone (Oxford, 1997), p. 157.

38 Daniel Rachel, *Isle of Noises: Conversations with Great British Songwriters* (London, 2013), p. 190.

39 Ibid.

40 Ibid. The original version of the song is in 9/8, although Johnny Cash recorded a later version in 4/4.

41 Rachel, *Isle of Noises*, p. 190.

42 *VH1 Storytellers: Sting*, VH1 (broadcast 15 July 1996).

43 Jonathan Harvey, *Music and Inspiration* (London, 1999), p. iv.

44 Ibid., p. v.

45 The practice of being inspired by classical literature arguably became more common during his solo career. For example, the line 'My mistress's eyes are nothing like the sun' (from the song 'Sister Moon') is taken from Shakespeare's Sonnet 130, while the album title *Ten Summoner's Tales* is inspired by Geoffrey Chaucer's *Canterbury Tales*.

46 'Bring on the Night' was originally part of the Last Exit song 'Carrion Prince'. Sting outlines how '[t]he second line was shamelessly lifted from

T. S. Eliot's 'The Love Song of J. Alfred Prufrock' (Sting, *Lyrics by Sting*, p. 30). According to Sting, 'Don't Stand So Close To Me' is loosely based on Vladimir Nabokov's *Lolita* (ibid., p. 40). 'Secret Journey' was inspired by G. I. Gurdjieff's *Meetings with Remarkable Men* (ibid., p. 70). 'Tea in the Sahara' is based on *The Sheltering Sky* by Paul Bowles (ibid., p. 90).

47 'Next to You', 'So Lonely', 'Hole in My Life', 'Can't Stand Losing You', 'The Bed's too Big without You' and 'I Burn for You' are examples of songs about Sting's love life. 'Man in a Suitcase' is an example of a 'travelling' song. According to Sting's book *Lyrics by Sting*, the vast majority of the songs on both *Zenyatta Mondatta* and *Ghost in the Machine* were written in the west of Ireland, while the songs on *Synchronicity* were written at 'Golden Eye' – Ian Fleming's old home on the north shore of Jamaica. He also regards the move in 1992 to his Lake House mansion in Wiltshire as inspiring him to write. 'Rehumanize Yourself' is inspired by the death of a 'young man kicked to death by a gang of skinheads near [his] home', a story which Sting watched on the news (Sting, *Lyrics by Sting*, p. 99).

48 Rachel, *Isle of Noises*, p. 194.

49 Ibid., p. 195.

50 Ibid.

51 In Andy Summers's *One Train Later*, p. 318, he recalls Sting reading Jung's autobiography *Memories, Dreams, Reflections* while on tour in North America. Jung also had a troublesome relationship with his father and, like Sting, was raised within the Christian faith, developed issues with it, was haunted by dreams and confessed to having a split personality, which Jung described as 'personality no 1 and 2'.

52 Sting, *Lyrics by Sting*, p. 33.

53 Rachel, *Isle of Noises*, p. 196.

54 Sting, 'How I Started Writing Songs Again' [video], TED 2014, March 2014, www.ted.com.

55 Ibid.

56 Ibid.

57 Ibid.

58 Harvey, *Music and Inspiration*, p. 5.

59 Ibid., pp. 5–6. Although the form of divinity is different, the concept of divine inspiration in art has a long history. For example, Homer's famous opening lines of *The Odyssey*, written approximately 800 years BC are 'Sing in me, Muse, and through me tell the story.'

7 POLITICS

1 Steve Turner, 'Pretentious? Sting?', *Q Magazine* (1987), available at www. rocksbackpages.com, accessed 10 July 2015, and Sting, *Lyrics by Sting* (London, 2007), p. 42.

2 Sting, *Lyrics by Sting*, p. 75. The house is now a hotel.

3 Sting and Andy Summers, 'Murder by Numbers', The Police, *Synchronicity* (1983).

4 Sting, *Lyrics by Sting*, p. 92.

5 Frank Zappa with Peter Occhiogrosso, *The Real Frank Zappa Book* (London, 1989).

6 The Police performed an impromptu performance at Sting's wedding on 20 August 1992, in addition to a performance at their induction at the Rock & Roll Hall of Fame in 2003.

7 Charles Bermant, 'A Conspiracy of Hope: Amnesty International' (6 June 1986), www.rocksbackpages.com, accessed 1 May 2017.

8 Ibid.

9 Ibid.

10 Ibid.

11 Ibid.

12 Ibid. The article goes on to discuss how many fans 'savoured the music but ignored the message'.

13 As a result of this tour, Reebok decided to place human rights more centrally in its corporate culture, establishing the 'Reebok Human Rights Award' in 1988. Aimed at honouring non-violent activists under the age of thirty, the programme closed in 2007. Unsurprisingly, Reebok's decision to make human rights a priority has received criticism, with one commentator regarding it as 'a PR tool . . . for executives to distract attention away from their own corporate human rights record'. See 'The Reebok Human Rights Award Spectacle', available at http://business.nmsu.edu, accessed 8 July 2015.

14 Sting, *Lyrics by Sting*, p. 126.

15 Ibid.

16 The performance of 'Don't Stand So Close to Me' is heavily influenced by the Godley and Creme remix of 1986.

17 Jack Healey, 'Kennedy Center Honoree Sting Deserves Highest Regard for his Work in Human Rights', *Huffington Post* (9 February 2015), www.huffington-post.com, accessed 9 July 2015.

18 N. A., 'Chile Honour for Star Sting', *The Mirror* (16 January 2001), p. 2.

19 Ibid.
20 Healey, 'Kennedy Center Honoree Sting Deserves Highest Regard for His Work in Human Rights'.
21 Ibid.
22 Ibid.
23 'Blondie and Bob Geldof Join Amnesty International Benefit', *Daily Star* (31 January 2014), www.dailystar.co.uk.
24 Paul Du Noyer, 'Stingtime in Paris – the Police Chief Sets Himself Free . . .', (June 1985), www.sting.com, accessed 1 May 2017.
25 Ibid.
26 When the poem was adapted as 'Jerusalem' by Hubert Parry in 1916, it effectively became both a hymn and a protest song.
27 Peter Butt, 'Notes and Queries: What Were William Blake's Dark Satanic Mills?', *The Guardian* (13 September 2012), p. 15.
28 Ibid.
29 Jessica Elgot, 'Margaret Thatcher Funeral: Easington Colliery Holds a Party', *Huffington Post* (17 April 2013), www.huffingtonpost.co.uk, accessed 8 July 2015.
30 In 'You're A Lady' (1972) and 'Matchstalk Men and Matchstalk Cats and Dogs' (1978) respectively.
31 See www.pophistorydig.com.
32 Larry Speaks, *Speaking Out: The Reagan Presidency from Inside the White House* (New York, 1988).
33 Nicholas Barber, 'Landscape of My Dreams', *The Independent* (6 November 1994), p. 15.
34 Pozner Vladimir Vladimirovich, interview with Sting [video], www.youtube.com, accessed 8 July 2015.
35 The 'high culture' link with Prokofiev was to be re-established in 1991, when Sting recorded the narrative for *Peter and the Wolf*.
36 Perhaps the most famous instance of Sting doing this occurred during his guest appearance on Dire Straits' 'Money for Nothing' (1985), which incorporates 'Don't Stand So Close to Me' towards the end, giving Sting a share of the songwriting credits. Two years later, this practice is continued on his next solo album . . . *Nothing Like the Sun*, which references 'If You Love Somebody Set them Free' during 'We'll Be Together'. Also in 1987, while performing live with the Gill Evans Orchestra, Sting quotes The Beatles' 'From Me to You' at the end of his performance of 'Little Wing' and 'Walking on the Moon' during 'Tea in the Sahara'.
37 Zappa with Occhiogrosso, *The Real Frank Zappa Book*.

38 'Reagan at Bitburg' successfully captures in musical form what Zappa saw as a reference to a verbally challenged president. See Frank Zappa, *Civilization Phaze III* (1994).

39 Christopher Gable, *The Words and Music of Sting* (Westport, CT, 2008).

40 Sting, *Lyrics by Sting*, p. 106.

41 Commencing with his personal protest on 'O My God', written during his Last Exit period, many of Sting's songs quote or paraphrase the Bible, sometimes subverting its original intent. For example, the title track from *All This Time* quotes one of Jesus's beatitudes 'Blessed are the poor, for they shall inherit the earth', before asserting that Sting heard his father laughing. The title track of *Sacred Love* also experiments with this irreverence, including two references from the book of Genesis: 'The Spirit moves over the water' and 'The Word got made into flesh.' The first of these is subverted by stating the Spirit is in the shape of a heavenly daughter. This is followed by a quote from the Ten Commandments ('Thou shalt not covet, thou shalt not steal'). The perspective of a distant God can also be found more subliminally in songs such as 'Why Should I Cry for You?' and 'When the Angels Fall' from *The Soul Cages*. Furthermore, Sting quotes the Bible in songs such as 'Mad about You' (which is based on the book of Samuel, Chapter Eleven), 'Jeremiah Blues (Part 1)' and 'Saint Augustine in Hell'.

42 Sting, *All This Time* [DVD], 2001.

43 Steve Turner, 'Pretentious? Sting?'.

44 Alan Jackson 'Change the Record Sting', *The Times* (30 January 1993), http://search.proquest.com.ergo.glam.ac.uk, accessed 30 August 2015.

45 Ibid.

46 Ibid.

47 Jeremy Clarkson, 'Hey Kids, Where Have all the Protest Songs Gone?', *Sunday Times* (26 November 2000), p. 15.

48 Ibid. This is a quote from the song, relating to the songwriter's feelings regarding the war in Vietnam, among other things.

49 Clarkson, 'Hey Kids, Where Have All the Protest Songs Gone?'.

50 Gavin Martin, 'Stung at Last: Gavin Martin Overcomes His Allergy to Sting to Admit He's Made another Decent Album', *Daily Mirror* (19 September 2003), p. 20.

51 Ibid.

52 Michael McCarthy, 'The Great Green Survey', *The Independent* (10 January 2008), p. 8.

53 Ed Pilkington, 'Sting Charity Criticised as He Marks 20 Years in Rainforest Activism: Watchdog Gives U.S. Branch Zero Rating 3 Years in a Row: Stars Join

Singer for New York Biennial Benefit Gig', *The Guardian* (7 May 2008), p. 18.

54 Jeremy Paxman, *Newsnight*, available at www.youtube.com as 'Jeremy Paxman vs. Sting Copenhagen 2009', accessed 15 May 2017.

55 Ibid.

56 Simon Neville and David Williams, 'Sting and the Tyrant: Human Rights Champion Jokes with Syria's Brutal Leader', *Daily Mail* (25 February 2012), p. 11.

57 Ibid.

58 George Lipsitz, *Dangerous Crossroads: Popular Music, Postmodernism and the Poetics of Place* (London, 1994), p. 56.

CONCLUSION: FROM AMERICA TO THE MAGNETIC NORTH

1 Sting, *Lyrics by Sting* (London, 2007), p. 84.

2 Ibid.

3 Sting, *Broken Music* (London, 2003), p. 320.

4 Jim Green, 'Police Lean to America', *Trouser Press* (February 1979), www.rocksbackpages.com, accessed 20 July 2015.

5 The song was originally released twelve months before, but failed to chart.

6 Green, 'Police Lean To America'.

7 Ibid.

8 Mick Brown, 'The Police Take to the Street', *Rolling Stone* (3 May 1979), available at www.rocksbackpages.com, accessed 1 May 2017.

9 Richard Grabel, 'The Police: Bottom Line, New York' (June 1979), www.rocksbackpages.com, 1 May 2017.

10 Ibid.

11 Susan Whitall, 'Police Report: Message From Three Bottle Blonds . . .' (February 1980), www.rocksbackpages.com, 1 May 2017.

12 Christopher Sandford, *Sting: Demolition Man* (New York, 1998), p. 103. Sting would continue to use the Caribbean to feed his creativity over the next few years, recording *Dream of the Blue Turtles* partially at the Barbados-based Blue Wave Studios, and then returning to Air Studios for . . . *Nothing Like the Sun* in 1987. After recording *The Soul Cages* between studios in Paris and Italy, Sting made a transition when working on *Ten Summoner's Tales* in 1993 and its follow up *Mercury Falling* three years later, recording both at the Wiltshire mansion he purchased in 1992 – Lake House. Sting was to continue this practice, recording parts of *Brand New Day* and *Songs from the Labyrinth* at his Il Palagio home in Tuscany, Italy, purchased in 1999. For many of these recordings, Sting utilized mobile recording technology, by simply importing

the technology into spaces in which he wished to work – be it at one of his homes, or in locations such as Villa Salviati in Tuscany, where much of *The Soul Cages* was recorded.

13 See www.sting.com.

14 Sting, *Bring on the Night* [DVD], A&M Films (1985).

15 See Tim Lawrence, *Love Saves the Day: A History of American Dance Music Culture, 1970–1979* (Durham, 2004), p. 374.

16 The song itself appears to be heavily influenced by Frank Zappa's 'Disco Boy' (1976). Left-wing punk bands such as the Dead Kennedys and The Slickee Boys had previously released 'Saturday Night Holocaust' (1978) and 'Put a Bullet thru the Jukebox' respectively.

17 See John Rockwell, 'Pop View; Rock vs Disco: Who Really Won The War?', *New York Times* (16 September 1990), www.nytimes.com, accessed 1 May 2017.

18 Chris Campion, *Walking on the Moon: The Untold Story of the Police and the Rise of New Wave Rock* (London, 2009), p. 83.

19 'Star's Parents Have Cancer', *The Journal* (8 December 1986), and Wayne Halton, 'Sting Flying Home to Visit Sick Parents', *The Journal* (9 December 1986).

20 'Sting Not Expected at Funeral', *The Journal* (23 November 1987).

21 Sting, *Lyrics by Sting*, p. 84.

22 Lennon wrote another song on the album dedicated to his mother – 'Mother' – in addition to the earlier 'Julia' (*The Beatles*, 1968). Bono has also written about his mother on an ongoing basis – see 'Mofo' (*Pop*, 1997) and 'Iris (Hold Me Close)' (*Songs of Innocence*, 2014).

23 Taken from 'The Lazarus Heart', . . . *Nothing Like the Sun* (1987). Birds on the roof are often associated with death, according to superstitious belief.

24 Vic Garbarini, 'Death, Rebirth, and this Business of Music – Sting on the Ties that Bind' (November 1987), www.sting.com, accessed 1 May 2017.

25 Ibid.

26 James 'Tappy' Wright and Rod Weinberg, *Rock Roadie: Backstage and Confidential with Hendrix, Elvis, The Animals, Tina Turner, and an All-star Cast* (New York, 2010).

27 Jackie Smith and Hank Johnston, *Globalization and Resistance: Transnational Dimensions of Social Movements* (New York, 2002), p. 125.

28 'Sting Exploiting Indians', *The Journal* (8 June 1989).

29 Sting, *Lyrics by Sting*, p. 143.

30 'And £10,000 for Town's Arts Centre', *Evening Chronicle* (10 January 1986). Having subsequently fallen into disrepair and closing in 2008, the venue was more recently reported to be undergoing a restoration scheme. The Buddle

Arts Centre event was followed by two nights at Newcastle City Hall, which, despite Sting's positive contributions, again had a negative narrative in the local press, who reported the concerts as being more than twice the price of 'normal concerts' at the venue. Aside from the Newcastle dates, the only concerts played in the UK as part of the early dates on *The Soul Cages* tour were in London – five nights at the Hammersmith Odeon, although Sting was to return in November, prior to the conclusion of the tour in February 1992.

31 Although Sting used the Newcastle showcases to get feedback on the script and to check the authenticity of *The Last Ship*, his New York events were more related to getting financial support. In retrospect, although it would have made more sense to have the premiere in Newcastle, it is presumed that the pre-Broadway events in Chicago took place in order to satisfy those who made financial contributions.

32 For an example of a positive review, see Rex Reed, 'Dream Boat: Sting's New Musical, "The Last Ship", is First-rate', *The Observer* (29 October 2014), http://observer.com.

33 Investors included Herb Alpert and Jerry Moss, the founders of A&M records. According to the *Wall Street Journal*, the show cost around $14 million to produce and earned $8,634,097 over its run. See Christopher John Farley, 'Why Sting's "The Last Ship" Stopped Sailing', *Wall Street Journal* (6 January 2015), http://blogs.wsj.com. For an example of a less-than-favourable review about the book by Logan and Yorkey, see Jeremy Gerard, '"The Last Ship" Review: Jeremy Gerard on Sting's Tuneful but too-familiar Broadway Show', *Deadline Hollywood* (26 October 2014), http://deadline.com.

34 Phil Sutcliffe and Hugh Fielder, *L'Historia Bandido* (New York, 1981), p. 23.

35 Ibid.

36 Joe Sharkey, *Akenside Syndrome: Scratching the Surface of Geordie Identity* (Petersfield, 2014), p. 5. The author of this book proceeds to describe Sting as 'the quintessential modern-day personification of Akenside Syndrome'. Sting's wealth is regularly brought up in Newcastle-based press. For example, an edition of *The Chronicle* discussed the recent sale of Sting's nine-bedroom home in Queen Anne's Gate, London, for £19 million, comparing this with the worth of his other homes to the typical house prices in the Wallsend area where he used to live. See Mike Kelly, 'Star Sees his Central London Home Go for a Song', *The Chronicle* (28 August 2015), p. 12.

37 Michael Dwyer, *Back to the Fifties: Nostalgia, Hollywood Film, and Popular Music of the Seventies and Eighties* (Oxford, 2015), p. 12.

38 Sting, 'Sting: If on a Winter's Night', YouTube, www.youtube.com, accessed

27 July 2015.

39 Ibid.

40 Sting, 'Sting: A Winter's Night Live from Durham Cathedral', YouTube, www.youtube.com, accessed 27 July 2015.

41 Hugh Barker and Yuval Taylor, *Faking it: The Quest for Authenticity in Popular Music* (London, 2007).

42 Ibid., p. 266.

43 Although punk is usually associated with working-class discontent, Tim Wall has pointed out that many of its leaders actually came from middle-class backgrounds. See Tim Wall, *Studying Popular Music Culture* (London, 2013), p. 53. For an account of how class can be performed as opposed to being an actual 'reality', see Nathan Wiseman-Trowse, *Performing Class in British Popular Music* (London, 2008).

44 Phil Murphy, 'Police Reject North', *The Journal* (14 October 1983), and 'Sting to Miss his Father's Funeral', *Sunday Sun* (22 November 1987).

45 John Hedley in conversation with the author, 12 June 2014.

46 Ibid.

47 Patrick Doyle, 'Inside Sting's First Rock Album in Decades', *Rolling Stone* (July 2016), www.rollingstone.com.

48 Ibid.

BIBLIOGRAPHY

Barker, Hugh, and Yuval Taylor, *Faking It: The Quest for Authenticity in Popular Music* (London, 2007)

Berryman, James, *Sting and I* (London, 2005)

Boone, M. Green, and J. Covach, eds, *Understanding Rock: Essays in Musical Analysis* (New York, 1997)

Campion, Chris, *Walking on the Moon: The Untold Story of the Police and the Rise of New Wave Rock* (New York, 2009)

Clarkson, Wensley, *Sting: The Secret Life of Gordon Sumner* (London, 1996)

Cochrane, Tom, Bernardino Fantini and Klaus Scherer, *The Emotional Power of Music: Multidisciplinary Perspectives on Musical Arousal, Expression, and Social Control* (Oxford, 2013)

Cohen, Louis, Lawrence Manion and Keith Morrison, *Research Methods in Education* (London, 2007)

Colls, Robert, and Bill Lancaster, eds, *Geordies: Roots and Regionalism* (Edinburgh, 1993)

Cook, Nicholas, *Music: A Very Short Introduction* (Oxford and New York, 2000)

Craske, Oliver, ed., *Punk Rock: An Oral History* (London, 2007)

Dwyer, Michael D., *Back to the Fifties: Nostalgia, Hollywood Film, and Popular Music of the Seventies and Eighties* (Oxford, 2015)

Gable, Christopher, *The Words and Music of Sting* (Westport, CT, 2008)

Harvey, Jonathan, *Music and Inspiration* (London, 1999)

Hebdige, Dick, *Subculture: The Meaning of Style* (London, 1979)

Hobsbawm, Eric, and Terrance Ranger, eds, *The Invention of Tradition* (Cambridge, 1983)

Inglis, Ian, ed., *Popular Music and Film* (London, 2003)

Laing, Dave, *One Chord Wonders: Power and Meaning in Punk Rock* (Oakland, CA, 1985)

Lawrence, Tim, *Love Saves the Day: A History of American Dance Music Culture, 1970–1979* (Durham, NC, 2004)

Lipsitz, George, *Dangerous Crossroads: Popular Music, Postmodernism and the Poetics of Place* (London, 1994)

MacDonald, Raymond, David Hargreaves and Dorothy Miell, *Musical Identities* (Oxford, 2002)

Marko, Paul, *The Roxy London WC2: A Punk History* (London, 2007)

Marshall, Polly, *The God of Hellfire: The Crazy Life and Times of Arthur Brown* (London, 2006)

Moore, Allan, *Rock: The Primary Text – Developing a Musicology of Rock* (London, 2002)

Perkins, Jonny, *In It 4 the Crack* (Gwent, 2012)

Rachel, Daniel, *Isle of Noises: Conversations with Great British Songwriters* (London, 2013)

Reed, John, *House of Fun: The Story of Madness* (London, 2011)

Russell, Dave, *Looking North: Northern England and the National Imagination* (Manchester, 2004)

Sandford, Christopher, *Sting: Demolition Man* (New York, 1998)

Savage, Jon, *England's Dreaming: The 'Sex Pistols' and Punk Rock* (London, 1991)

Sharkey, Joe, *Akenside Syndrome: Scratching the Surface of Geordie Identity* (Petersfield, 2014)

Shepherd, John, Michael Seed and David Horn, *Continuum Encyclopedia of Popular Music of the World: Media, Industry and Society* (London and New York, 2003), vol. I

Smith, Jackie, and Hank Johnston, eds, *Globalization and Resistance: Transnational Dimensions of Social Movements* (New York, 2002)

Speakes, Larry, *Speaking Out: The Reagan Presidency from Inside the White House* (New York, 1988)

Spicer, Mark, and John Covach, eds, *Sounding Out Pop: Analytical Essays in Popular Music*, Tracking Pop (Ann Arbor, MI, 2010)

Sting, *Broken Music* (London, 2003)

—, *Lyrics by Sting* (London, 2007)

Summers, Andy, *One Train Later* (New York, 2006)

Sutcliffe, Phil, and Hugh Fielder, *Police: L'Historia Bandido* (London, 1981)

Tagg, Philip, *Music's Meanings: A Modern Musicology for Non-musos* (New York, 2013)

Wall, Tim, *Studying Popular Music Culture* (London, 2013)

Wiseman-Trowse, Nathan, *Performing Class in British Popular Music* (New York, 2008)

Wright, James 'Tappy', and Rod Weinberg, *Rock Roadie: Backstage and Confidential with Hendrix, Elvis, The Animals, Tina Turner, and an All-star Cast* (New York, 2010)

Zappa, Frank, with Peter Occhiogrosso, *The Real Frank Zappa Book* (London, 1989)

DISCOGRAPHY

Sting Studio Albums
57th and 9th (A&M Records, 2016)
The Last Ship (A&M Records, 2013)
Symphonicities (Deutsche Grammophon, 2010)
If on a Winter's Night . . . (Deutsche Grammophon, 2009)
Songs from the Labyrinth (Deutsche Grammophon, 2006)
Sacred Love (A&M Records, 2003)
Brand New Day (A&M Records, 1999)
Mercury Falling (A&M Records, 1996)
Ten Summoner's Tales (A&M Records, 1993)
The Soul Cages (A&M Records, 1991)
. . . Nothing Like the Sun (A&M Records, 1987)
The Dream of the Blue Turtles (A&M Records DREMD 1, 1985)

The Police
Synchronicity (A&M Records, 1983)
Ghost in the Machine (A&M Records, 1981)
Zenyatta Mondatta (A&M Records, 1980)
Regatta De Blanc (A&M Records, 1979)
Outlandos D'Amour (A&M Records, 1978)

Strontium 90
Strontium 90: Police Academy (Pangaea, 1997)

Last Exit
[Bootleg], *Sting Last Exit Impulse Studio Demos* (Gypsy Eye Project, 2014)
'Whispering Voices'/'Evensong' (Wudwink Wud001, n. d.)

Newcastle Big Band
Newcastle Big Band (Wudwink/Impulse Organisation, n. d.)

ACKNOWLEDGEMENTS

I would like to thank the many friends, colleagues and acquaintances who have assisted with the research of this book – without your input, it would simply not have been possible. Firstly, thanks to all at Reaktion Books for giving me the opportunity to write it, in particular to John Scanlan for his excellent editorial comments and the proofreaders, who were amazing. Thanks to ex-Last Exit members Gerry Richardson and John Hedley, not only for giving time for interviews, but for responding to numerous email clarifications. Thank you also to the Creative Industries Research Institute at the University of South Wales for providing some early funding to enable me to work on the book. I would also like to thank other friends and colleagues, many of whom were involved in the Newcastle and London music scenes during the time of Sting's emergence, for their clarifications and guidance. In no particular order, these include David Wood, Andy Hudson, Mickey Sweeney, Lance Liddle, Marshall Hall, Rod Sinclair, Keith Nichol, Jeffrey the Barak, Ian Penman, Rik Walton, Sid Smith, Gordon Welsh, John Wilson, Christopher Black, Pete Loud, Peter Smith, Bill Robertson, Mick Proctor, Ann Dixon, Ken Potter, Tony Harris, Mike Finesilver, Jonny Perkins, Jez Collins, Jay Matsueda, Fabien Barral, Stephen Sayad, Toni Carbó, Gareth Hughes and Leah Mack (Sony/ATV Publishing). I would like to say a particular thank you to the following people: Ken Hutchinson, for providing invaluable ongoing assistance with Sting's early movements in Wallsend during the 1950s; Mike Howlett for offering his first-hand account of Sting's early years in London; Phil Sutcliffe, for providing great insight into Sting's movements between Newcastle and London; Lawrence Impey, for graciously providing his amazing 'Fall Out' photos; Peter Baylis, for giving me access to his fantastic early pictures of The Police; Dietmar Clös, for not only selflessly providing numerous photos and proofreading the 'facts', but for being a source of ongoing knowledge regarding 'all things Sting', and my friend James Crawshaw, for spending so much time scrupulously proofreading the entire first draft – thank you to one and all! As this book was going to press, novelist Tony Bianchi sadly passed away. Tony went to school with Sting and was a great source of information regarding the grammar school system Sting experienced. I considered Tony a fiercely intelligent guy and he provided some amazing insights into the constructs of Geordie identity. He will be greatly missed. Finally I want to say thanks to Sting, not only for meeting me in April 2015 and providing a great listening experience, but for helping me better understand my own complex relationship with my hometown. I hope the book helps others do the same.

PERMISSIONS

PHOTO ACKNOWLEDGEMENTS

The author and publishers wish to express their thanks to the below sources of illustrative material and/or permission to reproduce it:

Photos author: pp. 16, 21, 24, 65, 68, 82, 85, 111 (top), 127, 197; © Jeffrey the Barak: pp. 73, 79; © Peter Baylis/REX/Shutterstock: pp. 130, 138, 184; © Tony Bianchi: p. 29 (top and bottom); © Dietmar Clös: pp. 6, 189, 191; © Jez Collins: p. 133; © Mike Finesilver: p. 87; © John Hedley: p. 57; © Andy Hudson: p. 53; © Ken Hutchinson: pp. 22, 77; © Lawrence Impey: pp. 111 (bottom), 121, 134, 136, 139, 143; © Pete Loud: p. 153; © *The Newcastle Chronicle*: pp. 34, 156, 195, 201; © Jonny Perkins: p. 117; © Mick Proctor: p. 90; © Peter Smith: p. 69; © Rik Walton: pp. 48, 52.

INDEX